BIZARRE

TRUE CRIME

VOLUME 8

Ben Oakley

"Behind every man now alive stand thirty ghosts, for that is the ratio by which the dead outnumber the living." - Arthur C. Clarke.

Bizarre True Crime Volume 8

20 madcap and shocking true crime stories.

The Bizarre True Crime books can be read in any order. You don't need to have read the previous books to enjoy this one.

This is the first book of Season Two, and the eighth book in the series overall. There are seven books per season, released over the course of twelve months.

Season One: Volumes 1-7

Season Two: Volumes 8-14

1. The Real Amityville Horror

A haunted house, a violent history, an investigation by Ed and Lorraine Warren, dozens of movies, and the truth behind one of Long Island's most infamous family massacres.

2. The Real Hannibal the Cannibal

Known as the real Hannibal the Cannibal, Britain's most dangerous prisoner was confined to a specially built glass isolation cage in the basement of one of the country's most notorious prisons.

3. The Dead Crow and the Green Bicycle

A murder mystery involving a female victim, bloody bird prints, a dead crow, a gun in a canal, a pea-green bicycle, and a 100-year search for the truth, in a case fit for Sherlock Holmes.

4. The Red Barn Murder

A sensational 19th Century murder, an illegitimate child, a supernatural dream, a shallow grave, an evil squire, and a red barn, make for one of the most notorious olde English murder cases.

5. Death of the Prince of Motown

Marvin Gaye helped shape Motown in the 1960s and went on to become one of the most influential American artists of all time – who was shot dead by his own cross-dressing preacher father.

6. Horror of the Kansas City Butcher

There is perhaps no serial killer more inhuman than The Kansas City Butcher, who inflicted such terrible tortures on his victims that the term 'monster' has never been so appropriate.

7. John Harrison and the Resurrectionists

Son of one U.S. President, and father to another, John Harrison lived a fruitful life until his death in 1878 – when his corpse was stolen by resurrectionists within an hour of his burial.

8. Grand Theft Auto Crime Spree

Inspired by Grand Theft Auto, a man went on a nine-hour crime spree that involved carjacking, robbery, assault, theft of weapons, fraud, impersonation of a female, and pooing on a lawyers desk.

9. Deep Freeze Murder Mystery

A teenage girl is abducted, only for her body to show up a month later frozen like ice, but there are no fingerprints and no suspects, leading to one of Britain's most baffling unsolved murder mysteries.

10. The Devil's Night Murder of Martha Moxley

The night before Halloween in Belle Haven, a wealthy teenage girl was murdered in the night. The case went unsolved for 25 years, until a suspect was arrested – who had ties to the Kennedy family.

11. The Casino Killer and the Bad Samaritan

A teenager killed a young girl in a casino restroom and pushed her body into the toilet, minutes after his friend walked in on the attack – and did nothing.

12. The Eyeball Eater

The case of a crazed man who slaughtered his entire family, cut open their chests, removed their hearts, and gouged out his own eyeballs – before eating one of them.

13. The Ossett Exorcist Murder

A loving husband, thought to be possessed by 40 demons, became the subject of an all-night exorcism, and less than two hours later; ripped his wife and dog to pieces with his bare hands.

14. Case of the Missing Nun

While out shopping, a nun from a convent in Wales vanished without a trace, leading to an enduring mystery that has never been solved, and yet she wasn't the only nun who disappeared that year.

15. The Beasts of Satan

Bonded by their love of death metal and occult rituals, the Beasts of Satan went on a six-year killing spree involving sacrificial murder, drug-fuelled sex, and Satanism.

16. The Mormon Manson

A polygamous cult leader ordered the murders of at least 25 people, many from beyond the grave, in a tale of fear, control, and a mission to create the Kingdom of God on Earth.

17. Angel's Landing Cult

An evil cult leader, claiming to be an angel, slept with children to fix them and keep himself alive, and collected life insurance policies when his followers began dying in suspicious accidents.

18. Justice For All

When an abused woman reported her partner to police for assault, she never expected to become instrumental in solving the murder of a young girl twenty years earlier.

19. Halloween Murder of Collette Aram

A confident killer murdered a 16-year-old girl and escaped justice for 25 years until advancements in DNA technology captured him, in the first case to be profiled on Crimewatch.

20. The Bank Robber and the ATM

Dressed in camo gear but forgetting to put his mask up, a robber held up a bank for $150 before depositing the three-figure haul into his account – via the ATM outside the same bank.

The Real Amityville Horror

A haunted house, a violent history, an investigation by Ed and Lorraine Warren, dozens of movies, and the truth behind one of Long Island's most infamous family massacres.

I n 1977, American author Jay Anson wrote a book called *The Amityville Horror: A True Story*. He based the book on the real-life experiences of George and Kathleen Lutz, who claimed to have been terrorised by paranormal happenings at their house in Amityville, Long Island, New York, in 1975.

The book was made into an independent horror film in 1979, simply titled *The Amityville Horror*. It was the largest independent film of the time, grossing almost $90million at the box office and becoming the second largest film of the year behind *Kramer vs. Kramer*.

Then, as the sequels began to drop, something unusual began to happen. From 2016, small independent horror films began adding 'Amityville' to their titles to capitalise on the brand recognition, but many had no connection to the original book or film.

At the time of writing, there have been 42 films released based on the story of Amityville and using the original title as a stepping-on point. Those include 10 official sequels and a raft of VOD (video-on-demand) titles, including *Amityville in the Hood*, *Amityville in Space*, and – *Amityville Vibrator!*

In 2021 alone, there were six Amityville films released on an unsuspecting public. Despite the paranormal experiences of the Lutz family being the basis of the films, the true story behind the Amityville Horror is far less sensational but still haunts the town to this day.

Only one truth remained

Before the Lutz family made Amityville famous for all the wrong reasons, in 1974, Ronald DeFeo Jr. shot and killed his entire family as they slept in their beds. The location; 112 Ocean Avenue, Amityville, Long Island, New York, the same house where the Lutz family later experienced the horrors.

Just as the movies have confused the original story of the Amityville Horror, so too did Ronald, who changed his story over the murders multiple times. First, someone had broken into the house and killed everyone, then it was a mafia hitman, voices in his head, and his sister who he killed in a struggle.

Whatever version of the story came out, only one truth remained. In the early hours of 13th November 1974, 23-year-old Ronald awoke from his sleep, grabbed his .35 calibre rifle, walked through the house and opened fire.

He shot dead his parents, Ronald DeFeo Sr., 43, and Louise DeFeo, 43, his two sisters Dawn, 18, Allison, 13, and two brothers, Marc, 12, and John, 9. The family had owned the property since 1965 after moving to Long Island from Brooklyn where Ronald was born.

Later that evening, at around 6.30pm, Ronald walked into Henry's Bar in Amityville and told anyone who listened that his parents had been shot and that he needed help. The bar was Ronald's local, and his friend Joe Yeswit was inside, who informed Suffolk County Police about the possible shooting.

When they arrived at the house, they found the bodies of all six family members in their bedrooms, face down on the bed. Ronald's parents had been shot twice and his siblings killed with a single bullet to the head. Later autopsies suggested that his mother and sister, Dawn, were alive at the time of the attacks.

Confession

When Ronald told police he suspected the killings might have been carried out by a mafia hitman, he was taken into custody for his own protection. He claimed the hitman was Louis Falini, a local man considered to have connections to the mob but Falini had an alibi showing he was not in Amityville at the time of the shootings.

It would also have been considered unusual for a mafia hitman to have killed someone in their own home, let alone their entire family. When police realised that Ronald was deflecting attention away from himself, they uncovered inconsistencies in his story.

The next day, Ronald confessed to the murders and was escorted back to the house to show investigators how he had killed his family. He claimed the whole incident went by so fast that he couldn't remember all of it.

Ronald took investigators to the locations where he had discarded his bloody clothes and where he had thrown the rifle into the nearby river. He explained how he had taken a bath after the killings, changed into his work clothes and gone to work at the family's car dealership that same day.

While there, Ronald phoned the house wondering why his father hadn't turned up for work. When there was no answer, he left and hung out with friends, telling them that he couldn't reach his family on the phone – an attempt at creating an alibi for the resulting investigation. When he returned to the house in the evening to find his family dead, he ran to Henry's Bar calling for help. It was an unusual way to have admitted to the murders and more unusual that he had gone to work straight after.

Forged in aggression

The answer to the question of why Ronald had killed his family, lay hidden away in his past. Born 26th September 1951, the firstborn to his parents, he grew up in Brooklyn, New York, and got the nickname 'Butch' due to his size and reputation of fighting with other children and people bigger than himself.

His father was a highly successful car salesman who had worked at his own father's Buick dealership since childhood. As such, he could afford a lavish lifestyle for his family. But the lavishness and middle-class living came at a price.

Ronald Sr. was aggressive and sometimes violent towards his wife and children, with particular attention and abuse aimed at Ronald Jr. who was expected to have followed in his father's footsteps but didn't.

Along with being the target of aggression and physical abuse, Ronald was also bullied at school for the way he looked, though there wasn't anything entirely wrong with him, just that he was larger and meaner than some of the other boys.

During his teenage years, Ronald fought back and lashed out at his schoolfriends and family, even physically attacking his father. When his parents took him to see a psychiatrist, it made Ronald worse, and he would constantly deny that he needed help. Then, in 1965, the family moved to Amityville.

Violence and threats

To placate his violent manner, Ronald's parents showered him with gifts to incentivise good behaviour. When he was 16, he was gifted a speedboat worth $15,000 at the time. However, the appeasements made Ronald worse, and by the age of 17, he was addicted to taking LSD and heroin, two drugs considered the most damaging to an already broken mind.

Still believing they were helping Ronald, his parents continued to bribe him with gifts, including a job at the car dealership. He was also gifted a brand new car, guns, alcohol, and a weekly allowance from his father which he spent on drugs.

At one point during a hunting trip in early 1974, Ronald threatened his friend with the rifle he would later use to kill his family then acted as if nothing had happened, devoid of emotion or recompense. A few weeks later, Ronald interrupted a fight between his parents and pointed the rifle at his father.

When he pulled the trigger, the rifle malfunctioned but his parents were shocked to the core that their son had attempted to kill his father. It was perhaps an unfortunate foreshadowing of the horrors to come.

In October 1974, one month before the murders, Ronald planned a fake robbery with his friend. Ronald had been trusted with taking the car dealership's earnings to the bank, and in late October was due to transport $20,000.

Instead of going to the bank, he and his friend got into a mock fight and 'robbed' the money, which they split 50/50. When police arrived at the dealership, Ronald refused to help their investigation, leading his father to suspect that Ronald was the culprit.

Two weeks before the murders, Ronald threatened to kill his father if he continued to involve police in the robbery. Then, on 13th November, Ronald rampaged through the house and shot dead his entire family.

Voices in his head

One year later in October 1975, Ronald's trial began as his defence put forward an insanity plea. While on the stand, Ronald told the court he'd heard voices in his head that told him to shoot his entire family.

The defence psychiatrist concluded that Ronald was suffering from Dissociative Identity Disorder (DID) and was unable to fully connect with reality. His memories, thoughts, and actions were detached which meant he found it difficult to function in normal everyday life.

DID is rarely associated with violence, but in 1975, it was a different story. We live in a world now where mental health is thankfully better understood and we have the knowledge that disorders require professional help and are not bound to historical sensationalist ideals.

But the prosecution psychiatrists posited a different side to Ronald. They claimed that he had an antisocial personality and was only disconnected from reality due to his extreme use of LSD and heroin. They concluded that Ronald was aware of his actions which existed only to serve his own selfish reality.

The jury in the trial agreed with the prosecution psychiatrists and found Ronald guilty of six counts of murder. In November 1975, Ronald was handed down six consecutive life sentences.

In the years that followed, away from the sensationalism of The Amityville Horror, the case of Ronald DeFeo became even weirder. The biggest question on the lips of journalists and researchers was why. Why did Ronald kill his entire family?

No gunshots were heard

It was no secret that he had a poor relationship with his father and that a plausible motive was to kill him out of anger or revenge. Yet, it didn't explain why Ronald had killed his entire family, including his nine-year-old brother.

All six victims were found face down on their beds and had not been moved after their deaths. Ronald walked through the house with a loud rifle, so it remained unusual that the rest of the family didn't wake up after the first victim was shot.

There was a suspicion that Ronald had drugged them but autopsies showed no signs of anything untoward. The rifle used in the attack had no sound suppressor which meant it would have been loud, with eight bullets used in total.

None of the neighbours heard gunshots with only one claiming they heard the DeFeo's dog barking in the middle of the night. It would have been odd to hear a dog bark and not hear the sound of a rifle going off eight times.

It was suggested that Ronald killed his father for his life insurance and killed his mother so that he would be next in line as the eldest child, but it didn't explain why his four siblings had to die. Then as time went on, Ronald told interviewers three new stories of what he believed really happened.

Tall tales of murder

In a 1986 interview from behind bars, Ronald said that his 18-year-old sister Dawn killed their father. Upon seeing what she had done, their mother killed Dawn and the rest of Ronald's siblings. When she tried to kill Ronald, he fought back and killed her.

In 1990, Ronald's defence team filed an appeal on the basis of a new story that Ronald had told. He alleged that he was now telling the truth as it was time for the world to hear what really happened and who he had been protecting.

On that fateful night, Ronald claimed an unidentified attacker, who was known to Dawn, killed their parents. Dawn then walked through the house and killed the other three siblings, before turning the gun on Ronald.

Ronald saw the unidentified man flee the house as he and Dawn fought for control of the gun. The gun went off by accident and killed Dawn. Realising what he had done, he positioned the bodies on the bed and tried to come up with a false alibi to protect himself and his dead sister. He stated that he lied, simply to protect his sister.

The appeal was thrown out as the judge found it to be fanciful and full of lies, in attempt to place blame on a long-dead sister who by any account was an innocent victim. And then in 2000, a third story about what 'really' happened, emerged.

The most haunted house in America

26 years after the murders, Ronald was interviewed by author and researcher Ric Osuna. He told Osuna that he was guilty of the murders but that he killed his family in league with Dawn and two of her friends, because their father was plotting to kill him.

When Dawn murdered the other siblings, Ronald became enraged and knocked Dawn out before shooting her in the head. The two people with Dawn had by that point apparently left the house. Forensic experts have since debunked all three stories on the basis of evidence found at the scene.

Ronald died of natural causes in March 2021, with some outlets refusing to release the cause of death, most likely to continue the sensationalist circus built upon the paranormal happenings written about in The Amityville Horror.

In December 1975, one year after the murders and one month after Ronald's conviction, the Lutz family moved into 112 Ocean Avenue. After only 28 days, the family fled the house after being terrorised by paranormal entities.

Three months after they fled, in March 1976, the house was investigated by demonologists and paranormal investigators, Ed and Lorraine Warren, who are now immortalised in *The Conjuring* movies.

One of their images taken from inside the house shows a young boy with glowing eyes standing at the foot of the main staircase. It has since been used as proof that the house was haunted, whether by the ghosts of the DeFeo family or something far more sinister.

Some paranormal researchers, including the Warren's, believe that Ronald had been possessed by one of the house's demon spirits, and maintain it to be the reason why he went on to kill his family. The voices he heard were put down to possession.

Regardless of one's own beliefs surrounding The Amityville Horror and the DeFeo massacre that came before, the property is still considered one of the most haunted houses in the United States – with no vibrator in sight.

FACTS!

The Amityville House sold in February 2017 to an unidentified owner for $605,000, which was $200,000 less than the asking price.

Amityville is considered safer than 75% of other U.S. cities.

The population of Amityville has remained steady between 9,000 to 9,500 from the 1970s onwards.

The Real Hannibal the Cannibal

Known as the real Hannibal the Cannibal, Britain's most dangerous prisoner was confined to a specially built glass isolation cage in the basement of one of the country's most notorious prisons.

Considered one of Britain's most dangerous prisoners, Robert John Maudsley killed four people, three of them while in maximum security facilities. To protect other inmates, a special glass cell was constructed in the basement of HMP Wakefield which became known as The Cage.

Born in 1953, Maudsley had 11 siblings growing up and spent most of his time in an orphanage due to the broken relationship with his parents. When he was eight, Maudsley was physically and sexually abused by his parents.

He had been raped as a child and didn't escape the rotating door of abuse until social services stepped in and removed him from his parents' care when he was 10. His broken childhood led him to a deep drug addiction in his teenage years, which inevitably sent him down a spiral of self-abuse.

To subsidise his addiction, he turned to prostitution, and moved to London when he was 16. He attempted suicide on many occasions, which led to him receiving temporary psychiatric care, where he was diagnosed with a deep-rooted depression.

He told doctors he was hearing voices telling him to go back and kill his parents, which he later claimed would have been the right thing to do. *'If I had killed my parents in 1970, none of these people need have died.'* – Maudsley

In 1974, a punter named John Farrell picked Maudsley up for sex but he had darker fantasies he wanted to share with the then 19-year-old. Farrell showed Maudsley photographs of the children he had sexually abused.

Enraged by images of child abuse which had brought back memories of his own upbringing, Maudsley killed Farrell by strangling him with a garotte, stabbing him multiple times, and hitting him over the head with a hammer.

The brain eater

Not long after, Maudsley surrendered to police and asked for psychiatric help. It became clear to the authorities that Maudsley was not only a danger to others but to himself, having attempted suicide multiple times before Farrell's murder.

Because of his personal history, psychiatric issues, and extenuating circumstances, in 1977 he was found unfit to stand trial and sent to Broadmoor Hospital, a high-security psychiatric facility, which has been home to some of the country's most notorious criminals, including The Yorkshire Ripper, Charles Bronson, Ronnie Kray, and the Freddy Krueger Killer.

While there, he and another patient, John Cheeseman, locked themselves in a prison office with a known convicted paedophile, David Francis. They tied him up with electrical cord and tortured him over a period of almost ten hours, before Maudsley strangled him to death.

When they surrendered, one of the guards who was first into the room claimed that Francis's head had been cracked open and a spoon was sticking out of his skull. It was widely reported that a piece of his brain was missing, and that Maudsley had cannibalised it.

Though it remains a point of contention, it has never been conclusively proven either way whether

Maudsley had eaten part of the brain. As the story began to do the rounds, Maudsley earned the unfortunate nickname of Hannibal the Cannibal, despite reports to the contrary that the cannibal aspect of the killing was false.

Monster Mansion

Maudsley was convicted of manslaughter and not murder due to diminished responsibility but was deemed to be of relatively sane mind. As such, he was sent to Wakefield Prison, commonly known as Monster Mansion due to it's unfortunate roster of dangerous criminals.

Inmates known to have been resident at Monster Mansion include Harold Shipman (Doctor Death), Ian Huntley, Colin Ireland, Robert Black, Ian Watkins (former frontman of Lost Prophets), and USSR spy Klaus Fuchs, among countless others.

Other prisoners in Wakefield were already aware of Maudsley's reputation and he was given the nickname 'Spoons' due to the story of the spoon sticking out of Francis's skull.

On July 28th 1978, Robert Maudsley told other inmates that he was going to kill two people that day. His case is a unique one in that he would kill more people in prison than he did on the outside.

On that fateful day, Maudsley lured wife-killer Salney Darwood, into his cell. He tied a garotte around his neck and smashed Darwood's head repeatedly into the wall. He hid the body under his bed and tried to lure other prisoners into his cell.

When no one came in, he prowled the prison and walked into the cell of Bill Roberts before stabbing him to death with a shiv, a homemade blade. After having killed the two men, he calmly walked into a prison guard's office and placed the bloody handmade weapon on the table.

He looked up at the guard and said; '*there'll be two short when it comes to the next roll call.*' Maudsley surrendered to the guards and was transferred to solitary confinement to await trial, where he was convicted of both murders and sentenced to life at Wakefield Prison.

The cannibal and the cage

Maudsley had killed three people while inside a high security psychiatric facility and a maximum security prison. He was considered such a dangerous criminal that the prison service decided to build a unique isolation cage to house him.

In 1983, a specially-constructed cell was built in the basement of Wakefield Prison, where Maudsley has resided ever since. The glass cage, 5.5metres by 4.5metres, has bulletproof windows and an entire team of prison officers assigned to watch him.

In order to access The Cage you would have to go through an astonishing 17 locked steel doors. The only furniture is a cardboard table and chair, a bed made up of a thin mattress on a concrete slab, and a toilet and sink bolted to the floor.

The Cage, though rarely seen, has been likened to the Hannibal Lecter cell in The Silence of the Lambs movie. Thomas Harris, the author of the Hannibal Lecter series, wrote The Silence of the Lambs in 1988, five years after Maudsley's cage had been built.

He wrote the first Hannibal Lecter book, Red Dragon, in 1981, four years after the story of Maudsley eating part of a brain. Harris based some elements of the character of Hannibal Lecter on Maudsley's case, specifically the cannibal part of the story and the glass isolation cell.

Unsurprisingly, this led to Maudsley gaining the moniker of Hannibal the Cannibal in the British press, something which has never gone away. Maudsley is also known to have high intelligence and a passion for high art and classical music. Those who are allowed to be in close contact with him, have long claimed that he is a gentleman to be around, much like Hannibal Lecter.

An isolated life

Maudsley remains in The Cage for 23 hours a day and is fed through a glass drawer on the front. When he is allowed his one hour a day for exercise, he is escorted to the yard by no less than six prison officers and is banned from interacting with any other inmate.

Unsurprisingly, there are some people who see Maudsley as a hero vigilante, who killed paedophiles and wife beaters. There is still an active campaign to move him out of The Cage where he has resided for most of his life.

His family have long claimed that his isolation is detrimental to any rehabilitation and that he lives in a cloud of depression. In 2000, his defence team appealed to relax his solitary confinement measures or that he be allowed to end his own life with a cyanide capsule. Both were denied.

In the 1990s, notorious inmate Charles Bronson, who had also come from Broadmoor, decided to try and befriend Maudsley by sending him a watch via a prison guard. Maudsley told the guard to throw it out with the rubbish, leading to Bronson calling Maudsley an *'ungrateful bastard.'*

He went on to say that he hoped to one day bump into Maudsley and that he wouldn't need a blade to overpower him. He ended his tirade with, '*nobody rips my heart out or eats my brain, especially a nutcase like Bob Maudsley.*'

In 2010, Maudsley petitioned officials to let him play board games with guards to pass the time. His request was denied because of the murders committed behind bars, and the suspicion that Maudsley was still violent.

Their beliefs were backed up in March 2022, when the then 68-year-old Maudsley claimed in a letter to his nephew that he would kill again the moment he was released, and that he was content to remain in solitary confinement for the rest of his life.

Britain's most dangerous prisoner

There are some mixed beliefs as to whether Maudsley should be labelled as a serial killer, but by any classification, Maudsley *is* a serial killer. Whether he is a vigilante or not depends on how much one believes Maudsley had killed because his victims were child abusers or wife beaters, something which he hated.

Though some journalists and researchers write about the tragedy of Maudsley and how he was driven to kill out of revenge for the 'true' bad people in the world, it remains a fact that he has killed four men, three behind bars.

His childhood was tragic, forged in the darkness of abuse, lack of foundation, and hate over love. In his adult life, Maudsley chose to kill four others, whether out of revenge, hate, or circumstance.

Either way, he was deemed to be Britain's most dangerous prisoner and remains in the basement of Monster Mansion, feared by guards and other inmates. His case has shone a light on long term prisoners who wish to end their own life and if the law might be changed to allow it but there has been no progress since 2000.

No photo of Maudsley exists past 1983 and no images of The Cage have ever been released to the public. No one really knows if there truly was a spoon sticking out the skull of one of his victims but the legend perpetuates to this day.

If the prison service have deemed Maudsley dangerous enough to remain isolated in The Cage, and that Maudsley himself claims he will kill again if ever released, then maybe Maudsley is where he needs to be.

FACTS!

Wakefield Prison was originally built as a house of correction in 1594.

Harold Shipman, who was imprisoned at Wakefield, has the highest convicted murder count in the world, at 215 victims. He is suspected of killing another 65.

The most people killed in prison by another inmate is 47. The record is held by Pedro Rodrigues Filho, a Brazilian serial killer who actively sought to kill other criminals.

The Dead Crow and the Green Bicycle

A murder mystery involving a female victim, bloody bird prints, a dead crow, a gun in a canal, a pea-green bicycle, and a 100-year search for the truth, in a case fit for Sherlock Holmes.

I n a murder mystery worthy of an Agatha Christie novel, the unsolved case of the green bicycle captivated the nation and has continued to be written and spoken about a hundred years later, with many researchers putting forward their theories.

On 5th July 1919, 21-year-old Bella Wright was shot in the face and died of her wound immediately. She was found later that evening next to her bicycle. For months, the case made no progress until a bargeman discovered the frame of a green bicycle in a canal.

Bella was born in 1897 and was the eldest of seven children to a farmer and his wife. From the age of 17, she worked at a rubber factory in Leicester, just five miles from her home in Stoughton, where she'd lived all her life in a quaint thatched cottage with her large family.

Her cheeriness was infectious, and her love for life was admirable, and as such she became popular with the local boys, but she wanted a higher class of man. She met a Royal Navy engineer named Archie Ward, who worked on the HMS Diadem, a training ship based in Portsmouth.

They were engaged to be married but Bella was unsure if she would go through with it, and according to her mother, had fallen in love with another officer in the Royal Navy. There was local suspicion she was seeing someone else at the same time but the name remains lost to the annals of history.

Bella regularly cycled from her home to the factory and took the same route on most days, along the scenic Grand Union Canal in Leicester. It was on a lonely country lane near to the canal where her dead body was to be discovered.

A bloody crow

Alongside cycling to work, she also rode around the local villages, running errands, meeting friends, and picking up goods from shops. After one of the coldest winters on records, the warm summer of 1919 was most welcome and the cycling industry was starting to really take off.

On that fateful evening, Bella was cycling from her uncle's house near to the village of Little Stretton when she was killed by a bullet to the face. When the body was reported to police half hour later, they assumed she had died in an unfortunate accident.

In the dark of night, they moved the body to a nearby cottage while another officer went back to the scene. On the ground were bloody bird prints that led away from where Bella's body had been to the top of a nearby wooden gate. Beyond the gate in the meadow, a crow with bloody feet lay dead.

The long grass of the meadow had been recently flattened into a makeshift footpath that led away to the cornfields in the distance. Suspecting something untoward had gone down, the officer returned to Bella's body, wiped the blood from her face, and found a bullet hole below her left eye.

It appeared her death was no accident and they were dealing with a mysterious case of murder. The next day, the same officer returned to the lane and found a bullet pressed into the ground by a horseshoe. An autopsy revealed the bullet had passed through Bella's face and out through the back of her head, staining her straw hat with blood.

Mystery green bicycle

Within hours, witnesses came forward to claim they had seen Bella riding her bike next to a scruffy-looking man on a pea-green bicycle. They couldn't identify him but said he had been wearing a grey suit, grey cap, shirt and tie, and black boots.

Her uncle said she had left his house with a man on a green bike who she referred to by name but he couldn't remember what she had said. If the murder had taken place in today's world, forensics would have scoured the region en-masse, but 100 years ago, it was a different story.

All the police had to go on was the sighting of the man on the green bicycle, a dead crow, and crushed grass leading away from the scene. Six days later, as the police were still investigating the murder, Bella was buried at a funeral attended by hundreds of locals.

Soon after, the case went cold and Bella's death passed over into the unsolved – until seven months later. On a cold morning in February 1920, a barge on the River Soar snagged itself on an object on the riverbed, which turned out to be the frame of a pea-green bicycle.

Suddenly, police had what could have been a vital piece of evidence and reopened the Bella case file. Most of the serial numbers had been filed off but an expert reconstructed the number and tracked it to a bike shop owner in Derby who had sold it to 34-year-old maths teacher Ronald Vivian Light, nine years earlier.

Born in 1885, Light had a troubled childhood despite coming from a wealthy family. He was the son of a wealthy civil engineer who managed a coal mine. Light was expelled from Oakham School in 1902, aged 17, when he lifted a young girl's clothes over her head. He also admitted to sexual contact with a 15-year-old and was caught acting suspiciously around an eight-year-old.

A broken man

He went on to graduate as a civil engineer from the University of Birmingham, aged 21, and became employed as an architect and draughtsman at Midland Railway. He was fired from the job in 1914 when he was suspected of causing a fire and writing lewd comments in the toilets.

Light was also known to have forged military orders during his brief stint with the army following the outbreak of the First World War. He served for two years and was court-martialled when it was uncovered he had faked his own move orders.

He also deliberately caused a fire at a farm by setting light to the haystacks. None of the previous information was heard by the jury at his subsequent trial, which may have made a difference to the outcome.

While he was in the army, Light's father died by suicide, and upon returning home to live with his mother in early 1919, Light was provided with community psychiatric care. He claimed that the army had sent him home as a broken man.

At first, Light denied owning the green bicycle, then changed his story to say he had sold it to an anonymous buyer while he was in the army. Already suspicious of Light, police dredged the canal near to where Bella had been found. To their surprise, they found a brown leather army-issue gun holster.

There was no gun inside but there were bullets clipped away that matched the same bullet found beside the body. The holster was matched to the one Light was suspected to have smuggled from his army base. The police were then under no illusion that they had caught the suspect.

The trial of Light

The trial began in June 1920 with Light pleading not guilty. He was fortunate to be represented by one of the great barristers of the time, Edward Marshall Hall. The prosecution had a simple story in place as to what they believed happened.

They suggested that Light had been cycling along the same path when he decided to ride alongside Bella. He attempted to woo her but Bella rejected his advances. In a fit of rage, Light pushed her to the ground then shot her in the face where she fell.

The defence, led by Hall, posited Light's side of the story. Light had been riding beside the canal when he noticed Bella attempting to tighten a loose wheel. She asked him for help but he didn't have the right tools to assist her.

Realising she was headed in the same direction as him, Light offered to ride with her. He waited for her outside her uncle's house much to the bemusement of her uncle, who had asked Bella if she was okay, which she claimed she was. The pair rode off together along the country lane just before 9pm.

When they approached the junction at King's Norton, Bella told him that she was headed off on a different route and they parted ways. Light claimed to have ridden straight home and did not know about the death until three days later when he read about it in the news.

It occurred to Light that he was one of the last people to see Bella alive and it concerned him. Three months later, in October, he removed his bike from the attic, filed off the serial numbers, took it apart, and dumped it in the River Soar.

The prosecution took testimony from the maid of Light's mother, who stated that Light hadn't returned home until 10pm the night of the murder and had destroyed all the clothing he had worn throughout that day.

Two local underage girls also testified and claimed they had been accosted by Light three hours before the murder and that he had pestered them for sexual favours. They were riding their bikes close to the location where Bella was ultimately found.

No logical motive

The trial was being pulled in all different directions and the jury had a tough time on their hands. Hall managed to convince the court that a bullet fired from Light's gun would have caused a much larger wound and suggested the bullet had come from a high-powered rifle instead.

He went as far as stating there hadn't been a murder at all, and that Bella had been shot as a result of an unfortunate accident. She had ridden into the path of a hunter's bullet, by someone out shooting birds, which explained the bloody bird prints near the body and the dead crow.

Light admitted lying to police and agreed with witness statements that he was seen riding with Bella but denied being in possession or having used his army revolver. As with the green bicycle, he had thrown his gun into the river at the same time to avoid suspicion.

The prosecution cross-examined Light for five hours and he never contradicted himself. They also couldn't prove beyond reasonable doubt that he was responsible for Bella's death, as everything he was saying could not be disproved.

Yet, the biggest flaw in the prosecution's case was that they could not present a logical motive, instead hoping the circumstantial evidence would be good enough for a conviction. As such, on 11th June 1920, Light was found not guilty of murder and released as a free man.

Who killed Bella?

On the basis the jury didn't believe Light was the murderer, it suggested that they too had believed the tragic accident angle that Bella was hit by a stray bullet. Light slipped away to a new life after spending a few months with his mother and was known to have died in 1975 at the age of 89 in Kent.

The murder of Bella Wright remains unsolved and continues to fascinate researchers – and cyclists – to this day. In 2019, 100 years later, a 'green bicycle murder ride' took place along the route of the incident with events leading to the death recreated by period actors.

The only reason Light was suspected to be the killer was because of the green bicycle. Without the high-level of record-keeping by the bike shop owner, whose accounts and sales records went back over a decade, Light may never have been a suspect.

Which begs the question – was Bella murdered or was she the victim of an unfortunate accident? As it stands, there is simply not enough evidence to prove it either way. It seems unusual that a crow walked away from the body with bloodied feet, suggesting the crow was close by when Bella was shot.

Maybe Light was showing-off his shooting skills to Bella and tried to shoot a crow for her. When the crow descended a little too fast, he took a shot not realising he had fired in her direction. Perhaps Light deliberately killed her and in the end got away with murder.

Or maybe, an unidentified hunter was in the area and shot a crow at the same time Bella rode in front of it. The hunter may not have ever realised he had killed someone. Despite the theories, the case of the green bicycle murder remains a mystery that continues to divide true crime fans to this day.

FACTS!

In December 2021, Leicester had the worst crime rate in Leicestershire for bicycle theft, with 66 cases reported.

In 2021, Leicester reported 20,408 violent and sexual offences, one of the highest across England and Wales.

The village of Stoughton where Bella lived has a population of 351 (2010) and was home to the 15th Century *Stoughton Grange* before it was demolished in 1926.

The Red Barn Murder

A sensational 19th Century murder, an illegitimate child, a supernatural dream, a shallow grave, an evil squire, and a red barn, make for one of the most notorious olde English murder cases.

Ann Marten had not seen her stepdaughter, Maria, in eleven months and was becoming more and more worried with every passing season. Maria had supposedly eloped from the family home in Polstead, Suffolk, on 18th May 1827, to Ipswich, with her lover, local farmer William Corder.

Ann and her molecatcher husband, Thomas, would often write letters to Maria to find out what she was up to and to let her know they loved her. But Maria wouldn't reply, and whenever William returned to Polstead, he would give various excuses as to her absence and failure to respond.

He claimed that the mail must have vanished en-route, she had injured her hand, was busy with work, or that she simply forgot to respond. He assured them that their daughter was beyond happy in Ipswich and was always looking forward to seeing them again.

At around the same time, Ann had an unusual dream in which Maria was buried under the floor of the family's barn, half a mile from their cottage home. It was known as the red barn due to its heavy red brick roof.

Ann's dream haunted her waking hours, and after she had the same dream a second night in a row, she spoke to Thomas about it, who replied that the only way to allay her dream was to go to the red barn and examine it.

On 19th April 1828, though Thomas was superstitious of Ann's dreams, he went to the red barn to check it. Upon noticing a dip in the exposed ground, he dug deeper with one of his mole catching tools and he hit something hard.

Body in a sack

Thomas didn't have to dig much deeper to find the horror that awaited him. Two feet down, he uncovered a sack with the decomposed skeletal remains of a female body. He saw her long hair and found a green handkerchief around her neck.

Praying to God it wasn't his daughter, he fled the barn and ran back to the cottage, where he asked Ann if Maria had been wearing a handkerchief the day she left for Ipswich. Ann confirmed that Maria was wearing a green handkerchief that William had given her.

An inquest was held at a local inn, in Polstead, where Maria was identified by Ann. Though the body had decomposed, she was known to be missing a tooth, and her hair was recognisable, as were the clothing she had around her body.

The green handkerchief immediately implicated William in Maria's murder but he was nowhere to be seen. William had not returned to Polstead in many weeks and was found to have no connection to Ipswich. For a while, he had simply vanished into thin air.

William was born in 1803 and was two years younger than Maria when they met in 1826. He was the son of a local, wealthy farmer, and went by the nickname 'foxey' because of his cunning behaviour around other people, especially women. He was also a squire; a man of high social standing who lives on an estate in a rural area.

He wanted to grow up and become a teacher but his father refused to financially support him in his dreams and as such, William became a petty criminal to get money, selling his father's pigs, forging cheques, and stealing pigs from other farms to sell on. He was known as a menace around the village.

Out of wedlock

William's father sent him to London in disgrace after selling his pigs and refused to have anything else to do with him. But in 1825, his father asked William to return home, because his brother, Thomas, had died, having drowned while walking across a frozen lake.

Over the next 18 months, William's other two brothers and his father all died from tuberculosis, and William was left alone with his mother to run the family farm. In 1826, when he was 22, he began a relationship with the then 24-year-old Maria, who had fallen for his charms and his wicked ways.

She wasn't unknown to him, as she had previously been in a relationship with his brother, Thomas. They had a child together, but the child had died in infancy at around the same time he had drowned in the lake.

Maria had one other child from another relationship with a man named Peter Matthews, who wasn't involved in the child's upbringing but would send money on a regular basis to help her care for the child, who she had named Thomas Henry.

Maria became pregnant by William in 1826, and gave birth to their child in 1827, when she was 25. William wanted commitment, he wanted to marry Maria, to legitimise their child and relationship, as having children out of wedlock in the 19th Century was still considered immoral and punishable by public whipping.

But two weeks later, tragedy struck, when the infant died in Maria's arms. William wrapped the body in a box and buried it in an unidentified location. William insisted that they marry, despite losing their child, and wanted it to happen sooner rather than later.

An evil squire

William went to the Marten cottage and suggested they meet at the red barn where they could hide out before eloping to Ipswich. He was able to convince Maria and her mother that the local constable might be investigating Maria's third child out of wedlock but Maria stayed inside the cottage.

On Friday 18th May 1827, William stormed into the Marten cottage and told Maria that they had to leave at once. He claimed he overheard that the local constable had obtained a warrant to prosecute Maria and that if found guilty, she would face a public lashing.

Maria agreed to elope to Ipswich with him, and later than night, ventured out to meet him at the red barn. William had already taken some of her belongings and clothing to the barn so she could get changed before eloping.

It was the last time Maria was seen alive. William claimed he had moved to Ipswich with her, and when he returned to the village to check in on his mother, he lied that Maria was doing well, but couldn't come home because of the constable's warrant.

11 months later, Ann's dreams led them to the discovery of Maria's body, realising she had only made it half a mile from their family home. It was discovered that William had not moved to Ipswich and had instead eloped to London.

A local constable and a London officer tracked William down and discovered he was running a girls boarding house in Brentford, West London. He had married his new wife, Mary Moore, who had answered his advertisement for love in The Times and Morning Herald newspapers. William was arrested while boiling eggs in the parlour.

Public trial

William denied ever knowing Maria or the Marten family but the officers were convinced of his guilt and charged him with the murder. The trial began back in Suffolk on 7th August 1828, at Shire Hall, where tickets to the court were put up for sale due to the large number of people who wanted to witness the trial.

It was written in newspapers of the day that the judges and court officials had to fight their way through the crowds just to get into the building. William pleaded not guilty to murder, despite the mounting evidence against him.

He had motive, evidence linking him to the scene, two pistols that were purchased the day of the murder, his false claim of not knowing Maria, witnesses who saw him leaving the village alone, and Maria's ten-year-old brother, George, who had seen him with a loaded pistol the night of the murder.

It was initially thought Maria had been stabbed through the eye due to abrasions on the skull. The decomposed wounds on her body suggested she had been shot but the coroner could not rule out death by strangulation due to the handkerchief around her neck. The cause of death was listed as inconclusive.

The motive, they claimed, was because William did not really want to marry Maria and was doing so because she allegedly had heat on him due to his previous criminal ventures. The prosecution stated that it was enough of a basis to convict him on.

William, however, told a different story. He agreed that he was waiting in the barn for Maria but that he had left after an argument. While he was walking away, he heard a gunshot, ran back to the barn and found her dead with one of his pistols beside her, claiming she had taken her own life.

A body through the ages

The jury didn't believe him but modern-day researchers suggest they may have been influenced by the public's belief he was the killer. William was convicted of Maria's murder and sentenced to death by hanging and then dissection.

While waiting for the gallows, William confessed to the death but claimed he had accidentally shot her in the eye as she was changing her clothes. Only five days after the trial began, on 11th August, William was led to the gallows in Bury St. Edmunds, and hung at noon in front of thousands of spectators. He confessed to the murder moments before he was executed.

The body was taken back to the courtroom and placed on a table where his stomach was cut open, exposing his innards. Newspaper reports of the time suggested 5,000 people queued up to see the body of William Corder.

His body was sent to Cambridge University where it was dissected in front of students and experimented on with batteries to prove contraction of muscle tissue. Several death masks were made, with one replica still on show at Moyse's Hall Museum in Bury St. Edmunds.

William's skin was tanned by a surgeon and subsequently used as a book binding for an account of the murder and trial. His skeleton was put back together and used as a teaching aid which was put on display at the Hunterian Museum in London, until 2004 when it was removed and cremated.

There is a theory that Ann Marten was having an affair with William and they planned to kill Maria so they could be with one another. Her 'dreams' were revenge for William getting married to another woman, so she had sought a way to punish him by exposing Maria's burial site. It has never been proven but has remained a discussion point ever since.

The murder of Maria Marten at the red barn has remained in the public domain ever since and has all the elements required of a murder in 19th Century England. Surviving items involved in the trial are on display at various museums or have been sold into private collections.

In the 200 years since the murder, the story of the red barn has been immortalised in plays, poems, ballads, films, books, songs, and editorial articles. It is as notorious today as it was almost 200 years ago.

FACTS!

Maria Marten's gravestone was eventually chipped away to nothing by souvenir hunters and dark tourists. A sign on a nearby shed marks the place where it once stood.

Marten's Lane in Polstead was named after Maria Marten.

The Hunterian Museum is a museum of anatomical specimens in London, located in the building of the Royal College of Surgeons of England, and home to 3,500 specimens at any given time.

Death of the Prince of Motown

Marvin Gaye helped shape Motown in the 1960s and went on to become one of the most influential American artists of all time – who was shot dead by his own cross-dressing preacher father.

Marvin Gaye is perhaps one of the most influential American artists of all time and helped shape the sound of Motown from the 1960s onwards. His accolades include inductions into the 'Rhythm and Blues Music Hall of Fame', the 'Songwriters Hall of Fame', and the 'Rock and Roll Hall of Fame.'

Though his voice is still heard across the world, and his work continues to influence people to this day, many may not remember or even know that Gaye was shot dead by his own father following an argument in 1984.

It was a murder that sent ripples throughout the world of soul music and beyond, his death comparable with that of John Lennon and Elvis Presley, who were all featured on first class postage stamps for the Postal Service's Music Icons series.

It remains a point of sadness and bizarreness that Gaye's last words insinuated that he had wanted his father to kill him, telling his brother Frankie, '*I got what I wanted. I couldn't do it myself, so I made him do it.*'

Here, we take a deep dive into the bizarre death of Marvin Gaye and the events leading up to it, including abuse at the hands of his own father, theories of a planned suicide, and the loss of a legend known as The Prince of Motown. For the purposes of this story, Marvin Gaye is referred to as Gaye, and his father, Marvin Gay Sr., referred to as Marvin.

Abusive preacher

Born Marvin Gay Jr. in 1939, Washington, D.C., he added an 'e' to the end of his name to stop himself being bullied at school but his school life was the least of his worries. His home was where the true evil remained hidden from sight.

His father ran his home like a prison who frequently beat his son, starved his children and abused his wife, Alberta Cooper, in front of them. Marvin had already shown his dark side when he married the then 20-year-old Alberta.

She had a child by another man before they met but Marvin refused to bring up another man's child so he ordered her to send the baby away to live with her sister. When Gaye was born, Marvin took an instant dislike to him, believing that he wasn't really his child.

He refused to love Gaye in the way he would his other children and convinced Alberta that she should show less love to him. Despite his abuse, violent behaviour, and psychological torture, Marvin was a man of God.

He was a preacher at the Hebrew Pentecostal Church in Washington, D.C., and part of the church known as the House of God which advocated strict conduct and banned make-up, films, and TV.

Marvin was also an alcoholic and known womaniser who was later found to have had affairs behind Alberta's back and even had a child with another woman, despite his hatred against Alberta's first child, born before she had even met him. But his hypocrisy didn't stop there.

An all-powerful king

Gaye later described living in his father's house as *'living with a king, a very peculiar, changeable, cruel, and all-powerful king.*' Marvin forced them to quote bible verses from memory, with any mistakes punishable by severe beatings and whippings.

Marvin was known to enjoy wearing women's clothes and shoes and would sometimes deliver a hard whipping to Gaye while dressed as a woman. In response to starving his children, he claimed that their hunger would bring them closer to God.

According to his siblings, Gaye received the worst of the beatings and punishments, mostly because Marvin believed he was not his son. He would abuse Alberta whenever she gave attention to Gaye and went as far as accusing them of sleeping together – which they weren't.

Yet, it was Alberta who supported her son's talent in singing, while Marvin refused at every step of the way to back his son's endeavours. Gaye said in a later interview that if it wasn't for his mother, he would have taken his own life before he was a teenager, such was the brutality and hatred he received at the hands of his father.

Gaye achieved early success with *The Marquees*, who were a four-piece doo-wop band, founded in 1957 and operating out of Washington D.C. Other notable members included Bo Diddley, Billy Stewart, and Harvey Fuqua; the uncle of American filmmaker Antoine Fuqua.

Gaye moved with Fuqua to Detroit where he began a career as a solo artist. Within a decade, he was one of the biggest selling living artists on the planet, with the 1968 single 'I Heard it Through the Grapevine' going on to sell four-million copies.

And despite the rise to extraordinary fame, Marvin still hated his son and they never found any peace going forward. He despised his son's foray into the entertainment industry and resented him even more when he began making more money than him.

Suicidal paranoia

After a battle with alcoholism and cocaine abuse, Gaye returned to the big time in 1983 during the sold out *Sexual Healing Tour*. But the success of the tour led Gaye back to cocaine and into a veil of paranoia, instigated by the childhood abuse he had received from his father.

In August of 1983, he returned to his parent's home, a mansion he had purchased for them a decade earlier in Los Angeles, California, to look after his mother who was recovering from kidney surgery. His father returned to the home after a lengthy business trip in October that year, and for the next six months, Gaye and Marvin argued daily.

By late 1983, Gaye had become suicidal due to paranoia that someone was out to kill him and that he was being followed by stalkers, no doubt backed up by cocaine over-use, and a father who still ruled over him like a king. He was known to perform on stage wearing a bullet-proof vest.

In the days leading up to the murder, his parents argued to the point of Marvin becoming aggressive towards Alberta. Gaye stood up to his father and ordered him to leave his mother alone. Not liking being shouted at by his son, Marvin simmered through the night.

On 1st April 1984, shortly after noon, Marvin continued an argument about an insurance document that had cut him out. Gaye then pushed him out of his bedroom and began beating him up, throwing punches to the face and kicking him in the torso.

Alberta begged him to stop because Marvin had once told her if any one of his children laid a hand on him out of violence, that he would take up his God-given right to murder that child. Gaye left his badly-beaten father outside his own bedroom.

Minutes later, Marvin staggered to Gaye's bedroom, with a pistol that Gaye had given him for Christmas. He remained silent as he shot his son two times. The first bullet hit Gaye in the shoulder, and as he fell down, Marvin stood over him and shot him in the heart.

'I got what I wanted'

Gaye's brother, Frankie, was living in a guesthouse in the grounds of the mansion, when he heard the shots. He charged into the house and found Alberta screaming for help, before running up the stairs to Gaye's bedroom.

Frankie held his brother in his arms and heard his last words, which were, '*I got what I wanted. I couldn't do it myself, so I had him do it. It's good, I ran my race, there's no more left in me.*'

Police arrived within minutes and arrested Marvin who was sitting on the step of the front porch. They later found the gun under his pillow. Gaye was rushed to hospital but was dead on arrival, just one day before his 45th birthday.

The autopsy showed there were traces of cocaine and PCP in Gaye's system. PCP is known to sometimes cause the user to become violent and may have been one of the many reasons why Gaye was finally able to stand up to his father, albeit in a violent manner.

Marvin told the police he was scared of his son and kept the gun nearby in case he was attacked, which was allegedly something he feared. He also claimed he didn't know there were any bullets in the gun and had fired the weapon in self-defence.

He was held at a Los Angeles jail as the case was built against him. After having a tumour removed from the base of his brain, psychiatrists interviewed him to ascertain whether he was fit to stand trial. When they found him competent, the investigation got underway.

The Prince of Motown

In July 1984, Alberta filed for divorce, citing Gaye's death as the last straw of a violent relationship. Marvin's defence team filed a plea deal for a voluntary manslaughter charge, which was agreed by the judge due to the amount of drugs in Gaye's system and the injuries Gaye had inflicted on his father.

Marvin was convicted and given a six-year suspended sentence along with five years of probation. During the sentencing, Marvin claimed to have loved his son and reiterated that it was self-defence, believing Gaye could have killed him in the attack.

As the death had happened on April Fool's Day, many of Gaye's fellow artists and fans assumed news of his death to be a joke. As the world began to realise that Marvin Gaye had really been killed, there was an outpouring of grief, in what was referred to as a dark day in music.

In an unusual twist, Gaye's siblings believed his death to be a pre-meditated suicide. They claimed Gaye knew that by attacking his father, he would murder him as he'd always promised. That way, he could die without actually killing himself, which is what he wanted, and get his father taken away from his mother at the same time.

To this day, Gaye's siblings and friends are confident he had instigated his own death. By having his father carry out the act, it was the ultimate punishment Gaye could bestow upon him, knowing he would be haunted until the end of his days. Marvin died of natural causes in October 1998, aged 84.

In 1987, shortly after founding the Marvin P. Gaye Jr. Memorial Foundation, to help those suffering from drug abuse and alcoholism, Alberta died of bone cancer, knowing her son's legacy would inspire, help, and influence future generations.

Marvin Gaye's death shocks to this day and tributes are still paid to him across the world, through songs, music, and film. Like other music greats, his name rose above the bizarre circumstances of his death and moved into legend – as The Prince of Motown.

FACTS!

Marvin Gaye was blessed with a four-octave vocal range and started singing in church choirs from the age of four.

Gaye's music has appeared on soundtracks for hundreds of films and TV shows, including The Big Chill, Se7en, In Living Color, Remember the Titans, and Guardians of the Galaxy.

In 1971, Gaye signed a deal with Motown worth $1million, the most money ever paid out to a black recording artist at the time.

Horror of the Kansas City Butcher

There is perhaps no serial killer more inhuman than The Kansas City Butcher, who inflicted such terrible tortures on his victims that the term 'monster' has never been so appropriate.

This story is rather grim and contains descriptions of torture. It's included because Berdella remains one of the nastiest killers of the modern era and it remains bizarre due to the level with which he abused his victims and how he willingly carried out such tortures upon them.

On 23rd June 1987, Kansas, Missouri based serial killer Robert Andrew Berdella Jr. dragged a sedated 20-year-old Larry Wayne Pearson into his basement. He then violently tortured Pearson for the next six weeks before beheading him and dissecting his remains in August of that year.

Pearson was the last of six victims to fall foul to one of America's evilest killers, who would become known as either the Kansas City Butcher, Bob's Bazaar Killer (due to having a shop at a market), or The Collector (a film that influenced him to kill).

Berdella was the eldest son of a deeply religious family, with an Italian Roman Catholic father Robert Andrew Berdella Sr. and American mother, Mary Louise. Raised in Ohio, Berdella was sent on religious education courses and attended the local church for mass.

During his childhood he was afflicted with various impediments that saw him bullied in school and beaten by his father. When he was young, his father rarely allowed him to socialise outside of religious sermons and family chores.

As such, Berdella became a loner and was known to have been socially awkward. When he was five-years-old, he was diagnosed with near-sightedness and had to wear thick-rimmed glasses. Combined with a speech-impediment, he withdrew from society at an early age.

In doing so, Berdella didn't follow in his younger brother's footsteps and take up sport, instead becoming lethargic and gaining weight. Because of this lethargy, his father would often compare him to his younger brother, belittling him for not being like his other son.

The Collector

Although Berdella's father abused his children he would pay particular attention to his eldest son. He emotionally and physically abused Berdella, sometimes beating him with a leather belt around his genitals and buttocks.

As he reached his teenage years, Berdella became confused about his sexuality, which he kept to himself, and despite finding a girlfriend, finally came out as gay in his late teens. On Christmas Day 1965, when Berdella was 16, his then 39-year-old father died of a heart attack while at home.

Berdella turned to religion in the hope that faith would somehow see him through what he described as a difficult time, regardless of his father's abuse towards him. When he didn't find what he needed, he began reading up on other religions and soon started to lose faith in what he had been taught as a youngster.

At around the same time, he had turned his withdrawal into a mask of exaggerated confidence. He became difficult to be around due to his new rudeness and attitude towards others, believing himself to be superior to those around him.

Then he saw a 1965 British-American film called *The Collector*. In the case of Berdella, it was one of the first known instances of a movie directly impacting the thought processes of someone who had the potential to kill and would go on to kill.

The plot of the film is about a man who abducts women and holds them captive in his basement to add to his collection. It is a direct correlation to the exact process used by Berdella in his future murders, except that he chose men instead of women.

Berdella directly cited the film as an influence of how he could kill. The Collector was also said to have influenced the American serial killing duo Leonard Lake and Charles Ng., who together in the mid-1980s killed at least 11 people but were suspected of 25.

The pair built a bunker and a self-built torture-chamber in a secluded area of forest which became home to a number of elaborate torture machines to 'play' with their victims. But even their crimes paled in comparison to Berdella's

Preying on the most vulnerable

Two years later in 1967, Berdella moved to Kansas and went to the Kansas City Art Institute where he was known to have become a promising student, but things quickly took a turn for the worst. After falling in with the drug crowd, he started to abuse drugs and alcohol, and even began dealing to other students.

Some serial killers torture small animals in their childhood years, because of an ability to overpower small animals where they can't overpower human abusers or carers. Berdella started late and used art as an excuse for torturing animals.

As part of his art, he used sedatives on a dog to witness the effects, then tortured and cooked a live duck in front of other students – for art. After making notes on his experiments, he left the institute after widespread condemnation but no authority was contacted about it.

He was arrested a few months later in possession of Marijuana and LSD. It is unclear whether the LSD was the Orange Sunshine Acid which is the type that Charles Manson and other known criminals went on to use.

Orange Sunshine was created and sold by a group going by the name of The Brotherhood of Eternal Love, who operated at a Los Angeles beach resort. One of its dealers, Ronald Stark, had known connections to the CIA.

The same batch of Orange Sunshine was available four months later at a free concert held at Altamont Speedway. Four people died at what should have been a peaceful festival. One of them was stabbed to death by a group who had taken multiple tabs of Orange Sunshine.

Berdella stayed in Kansas and moved into the now infamous 4315 Charlotte Street, in the Hyde Park area of Kansas City. He enjoyed using male prostitutes and spent a lot of time in gay bars in the city, openly taking part in casual sexual encounters with other men.

He would spend time with drug addicts or homeless people and gain their trust by plying them with drink and drugs before allowing them to live rent-free in his home in return for sexual favours, some of which were forced upon the most vulnerable in society.

Bob's Bazaar Bizarre

Ever since his teens, Berdella realised the benefits of becoming pen-pals with foreigners. He wrote letters to people all over the world including Vietnam and Burma, two countries that were very much off-limits to the Western world at the time.

In return he would receive photos of ancient sites and small items from those countries, and so his collection began to grow. In disregarding mainstream religion he had developed a belief and understanding in alternative religions and occult magic.

This would lead him to open a rather unique store in 1982, a booth at the Westport Flea Market called Bob's Bazaar Bizarre, which was an antique and curiosity shop. It sold primitive art, Asian artefacts and jewellery, some of which had come from his pen-pals in Asia but much of it by stealing items to sell at the booth.

To subsidise his earnings at the flea market, which were constantly up and down, he started taking lodgers at his home and became friends with the son of one of his fellow booth operators, Jerry Howell. When Jerry was 19, on July 5th 1984, he became Berdella's first victim.

Berdella promised to give him a lift to a dance contest but instead drugged him with heavy sedatives, took him home and tied him to his bed. Over the next 24 hours, Berdella raped, tortured and beat Jerry, then abused him with various household objects.

Jerry died after the drugs stopped his heart and he gagged on his own vomit due to the pain of the abuse. Berdella then dragged the body to the basement to try and resuscitate him but instead suspended the body from the feet.

As Jerry's body was hanging upside down, Berdella cut his throat and other arterial veins in order to drain the blood. He placed a large cooking pot underneath the hanging corpse to stop the blood spreading across the basement floor.

A day later, he returned to the basement and used a chainsaw and knives to dismember the body. He wrapped the larger body parts in newspapers and placed them in several trash bags around the city, which were collected shortly after and taken to the landfill.

Acts of torture

We know all this in such great detail because Berdella had been keeping extremely elaborate notes and photographs of his victims and other assaults. His notes detailed each individual act of torture and abuse and outlined the intense physical and mental satisfaction that he gained from carrying out the murders in such a way.

If Jerry's murder was brutal then what followed was even more horrific. A year later in April 1985, 20-year-old Robert Sheldon begged to stay at Berdella's home after hearing how he helped people off the street.

Though Berdella initially agreed, he found Sheldon to be an inconvenience to his own lifestyle and drugged him before holding him prisoner in his bedroom. For three days, Sheldon was tortured in a variety of manners.

He was tied up with piano wire, had needles pushed underneath his fingernails, ears filled with waterproof sealant, eyes exposed to drain cleaner, and various parts of his body subject to burning and stabbing. Sheldon was suffocated to death after three days of torture and dissected in the bathroom.

In June 1985, Berdella lured Mark Wallace to his home where he was drugged under the pretence of providing him with a cure to his depression. He gagged Wallace then began torturing him in the bedroom. After needle torture and having an electrical device clamped to his nipples, Wallace died as his body went into shock – which frustrated and annoyed Berdella.

Three months later in September, Berdella met James Ferris who asked to stay at his home unaware of the torture chamber it had become. Like the others, Ferris suffered extreme abuse including being electrocuted until he couldn't sit up for more than a few seconds.

After extreme genital abuse and mutilation, Ferris's heart stopped and he died. He too was dissected in the bathroom. His fifth victim was Todd Stoop in June 1986, a man who provided sexual services in return for drugs – and Berdella was more than happy to oblige. Once again, Berdella drugged and tortured him.

Stoop was kept alive for two weeks and suffered horrendous pain from electrical shocks to the eyes, injections of drain cleaner into his vocal chords, and having his anal wall ruptured as Berdella forced his arm inside, causing him to die from shock.

The seventh victim escapes

Larry Wayne Pearson, the sixth and final murder victim, was one of Berdella's lodgers and Berdella hadn't planned on killing him. But after he bailed Pearson out of jail on 23rd June 1987, he made a crude remark about gay men, and Berdella saw red.

Berdella drugged him and dragged him into the basement – where the horror began. For the following six weeks until August 5th, when he finally killed him, Pearson was tortured and abused in the most horrific of fashions.

He would be injected with drain cleaner and had piano wire tightened around his wrists to cause nerve damage. Berdella broke one of Pearson's hands with an iron bar and electrocuted him with an electric transformer to all parts of his body.

He kept Pearson in various states of sedation and moved him around the house, including the second bedroom where he would rape and abuse him further. Towards the end, Pearson summoned the energy to bite Berdella's penis during a session of forced fellatio.

Berdella then beat him to death and later dismembered him in the basement. He stored Pearson's head in the freezer before burying it in the backyard. Although Pearson was his last murder, another victim escaped his clutches in March 1988, leading to his downfall.

22-year-old Christopher Bryson managed to escape from the house after three days of escalating abuse. When Berdella went to work, Bryson burned through his restraints and jumped from a second floor window, wearing nothing but a dog collar around his neck.

He broke his foot when he jumped but managed to cry out for help. Someone heard him and called the police, and Berdella was subsequently arrested on a search warrant after Bryson told them everything that had happened.

Inhuman

During the search of the property, investigators found 334 Polaroid images and 34 snapshot prints of his victims in various states of torture, before and after death. They found a human skull in the closet, a severed head in the garden, teeth in an envelope, and human spines in the hallway, though most of the larger body parts had been disposed of in landfills.

The basement was bloodstained and showed traces of flesh, hair, and brain matter. They found a chainsaw covered in blood with flesh parts in-between the teeth. But the main pieces of evidence used to convict Berdella were the detailed torture logs he kept on top of his cupboard.

In the summer of 1988, Berdella pleaded guilty to Pearson's murder and was sentenced to life imprisonment without the possibility of parole. He was also sentenced to an additional life term for the rape and assault of Bryson.

In September 1988, Berdella pleaded not guilty to the additional five murders. But his defence struck a plea deal that Berdella would plead guilty to one additional count of first degree murder, and four counts of second degree murder. The judge accepted the plea and sentenced Berdella to an additional five life sentences to run concurrently.

Investigators found a possible link to a total of 20 murders but only six could be verified using Berdella's notes and confessions. While in prison, he tried to convince interviewers and investigators that he had made mistakes and was not the demon he had been made out to be.

On 8th October 1992, while incarcerated at Missouri State Penitentiary, Berdella died of heart failure, much to the satisfaction of the family of the victims. Due to the widespread national attention the case had received, a local businessman purchased Berdella's home from the state and had it demolished as soon as he was in possession of the ownership papers.

Though we read many stories about the crimes of Ted Bundy, Jeffrey Dahmer, and Richard Ramirez among others, there is perhaps no serial killer more inhuman than the Kansas City Butcher, who committed the most atrocious acts against his fellow humans.

FACTS!

Kansas City, Missouri, consistently stays in the top 10 most dangerous cities in the United States. St. Louis, also in Missouri, regularly sits at number one on the list.

Kansas City, Missouri, has a metro population of 2.4million (2020), while the state of Missouri is home to 6.1million.

There is also a Kansas City in the state of Kansas (to confuse you) with a population of 156,000 (2020). The state of Kansas is home to 2.9million people.

John Harrison and the Resurrectionists

Son of one U.S. President, and father to another, John Harrison lived a fruitful life until his death in 1878 – when his corpse was stolen by resurrectionists within an hour of his burial.

J ohn Scott Harrison holds an esteemed place in United States political history as he was the father and son of two U.S. Presidents without being a president himself. His father, William Henry Harrison was the ninth U.S. President, and his son Benjamin Harrison was the 23rd.

Born in 1804, John fell into the political arena from an early age and became an Ohio congressman but wanted to follow his passion for farming. Due to his kind nature he was sometimes referred to as the gentleman farmer.

He married twice and had 13 children from both marriages, including future president Benjamin Harrison who lived to the age of 67 and died of pneumonia in 1901. John lived to a good age and died in his sleep on 25th May 1878.

His body was interred at a cemetery in North Bend, Ohio, four days later. The funeral attracted a wide range of landowners and politicians but they all noticed something untoward in the cemetery – a grave belonging to Harrison family friend Augustus Devin had been dug up.

At first, it was suspected that wild hogs were responsible for digging up the grave but it seemed unlikely. Benjamin, who was 11 years away from becoming president, and his two brothers, John Jr. and Carter, became concerned over the sight of the dug up grave.

John's grave had been walled with bricks but his children didn't want their father's body turning up on the outside of his coffin, so they ordered the grave to be reinforced with large stone slabs and cement before filling it in with soil.

His children paid the cemetery watchman a large sum of $30 to stand watch over the grave for 30 days in case the scourge of the graverobbers came to visit. Little did they know that their father's body was about to be taken.

The resurrectionists

Graverobbing in the 19th Century was booming, as the body chop-shop industry was worth a fortune to the right people. It was becoming so much of a problem that police would constantly be visiting medical schools and colleges to check if they were following proper methods for securing a body.

Even today, most medical schools and universities still require cadavers in order to train future medical professionals. The bodies are generally acquired when people die in public institutions and have previously agreed to their body being used for medical or scientific purposes.

The day after the funeral, John Jr. and his cousin George Eaton, accompanied by three Cincinnati police officers and a search warrant, arrived at the Medical College of Ohio, which had previously been in trouble for acquiring cadavers through illegal methods.

They went there to look for the body of Augustus Devin, as the sight of the dug up grave had haunted them both through the night, and they wanted to put on a show of power at the college to dissuade them from going near their father's grave, if they were still up to no good.

The medical schools around the country needed more bodies than the public institutions could provide and would sometimes turn to the black market for their needs. Although considered a serious crime, graverobbing was an extremely lucrative business.

So competitive was the graverobbing industry that many colleges stockpiled bodies for when they needed them. They paid criminals called 'Resurrection Men' who would get them the bodies they required, collectively known as 'The Resurrectionists.'

Human chop-shop

When John Jr. entered the medical college with his cousin and police, they couldn't help but notice the smell of the inner buildings, a lingering aroma of rotten flesh and old blood. They were escorted through the building by the janitor rather than a medical professional.

In the cellar of the building, they found a door connecting to a nearby alley and a shaft where bodies were lifted to the upper levels of the building using a winch. Up above on the highest level, there seemed to be a body hanging from the winch hook.

As they walked past a training room, they witnessed a medical student cutting off the breasts and head of a black women. They horrifyingly referred to the scene as someone 'chipping away' at another human.

In another room was the body of a baby on a medical table with no security, meaning the body was accessible to anyone. The janitor became worried that the group were seeing too much and went to inform the managers of the institute.

The team followed him to the upper levels of the building where they spotted the top of the shaft used to winch bodies up. Realising there was a body hanging off the hook, the lead officer turned the crank and slowly pulled up the corpse of a naked man, who had already been partially dissected.

When the cloth covering his face was removed, John Jr. almost fainted and had to be held up. In front of them, hanging from the hook of the winch, was not Augustus Devin, but his own father, who he had buried less than 24 hours earlier.

Stealing bodies to order

The resurrection men had been spying on the funeral from a hidden viewpoint and watched as the extra measures were taken with the stone slabs and concrete. When the mourners left, they removed the smaller stone slabs at the foot of the coffin and drilled through the wood.

They made a big enough gap to tie a rope around John's feet and pull him from the grave with ease, breaking some bones in the process. Incidentally, the watchman who had been paid handsomely hadn't seen anything as he claimed he was going to start watching the grave that night when it was filled in.

No one had expected the body to be stolen within an hour of the funeral, not least John's family. The next day, the local newspapers ran the story which soon made the national press. Unsurprisingly, there was public outrage at the concept of stealing bodies to order.

The fact that it was a member of the beloved Harrison heritage made matters worse. On 1st June, the Dean of the college and American physician Roberts Bartholow released a statement on behalf of the institute.

In it, he claimed the college had no knowledge of the theft and did not pay resurrectionists to source bodies for them. But of course, this was the same physician who only four years earlier had killed a female patient in an experiment by inserting electrode rods into her brain.

The Harrison Horror

Benjamin Harrison took offence to the notion that the college denied paying grave robbers and wrote an angry response to the statement in the newspapers the next day. He claimed that his father's corpse had already been experimented on by medical experts.

He refused to believe that the medical professionals who saw the body did not know it was John Harrison, who had been buried the same day. No one in the college seemed to know who had hung John's body from the hook, and everyone seemed to deny it had happened.

Clearly, a cover-up was already underway, and the person who was ultimately responsible for paying off the resurrectionists was never found, though many suspect it to have been Bartholow.

Benjamin filed a lawsuit against the college which was unfortunately lost to the corridors of time when in 1884, the courthouse was set alight and burned to the ground, with all its files and paperwork turned to ash. Five years before Benjamin became president.

The press referred to the case as the Harrison Horror, and the intense public interest led to various states passing new Anatomy Acts. It increased fines for graverobbing and allowed medical schools and colleges to use unclaimed bodies.

Unclaimed bodies were those people who died in public institutions and had no family to claim them, such as orphans, mental patients, prisoners, or those considered poor, which inevitably led to further abuse of the system when institutes began paying resurrectionists to 'create' their own corpses.

Graverobbing carried on into the early decades of the 20th Century and continues today in some parts of the world. Incidentally, Augustus Devin's body was later found in a large container of brine, being pickled at the University of Michigan.

FACTS!

To avoid detection, early graverobbers would not remove the whole coffin. They would hoist the body out by its head or feet, throw the clothes back in, and flatten the ground on top of it.

The New York Doctor's Riot of 1788 was caused when the New York Hospital began digging up graves for corpses, leading to a riot that left an estimated 20 people dead.

In March 1978, Charlie Chaplin's body was dug up and held for ransom in Switzerland. The body was recovered a couple of months later and reburied in concrete to stop it happening again.

Grand Theft Auto Crime Spree

Inspired by Grand Theft Auto, a man went on a nine-hour crime spree that involved carjacking, robbery, assault, theft of weapons, fraud, impersonation of a female, and pooing on a lawyers desk.

Sunday 25th March 2012 started out like any normal day in the south-eastern region of the United States. It was a warm evening in Kentucky when 25-year-old William Christopher Todd boarded a Greyhound bus to Tennessee for a day trip, with his red ponytail high on his head.

The bus was packed with travellers, locals, and families, headed to the Volunteer State with various stops along the way. At 3am on Monday 26th, the bus pulled in for a scheduled nine-hour stop in Nashville.

And then, for some reason, instead of resting up on the bus or checking into a motel, Todd went on a crime spree that remains unmatched to this day. By lunchtime on the Monday, Todd had racked up a total of 11 different offences as he went on his very own Grand Theft Auto rampage.

In less than nine hours, Todd burned down a haunted house attraction, tased drinkers leaving a bar, carjacked three taxis, crashed one of them, stole weapons, bought food at Walmart with a stolen credit card, pooed on a lawyers desk, and hid in a shopping mall's cooler tank.

The Slaughterhouse

No one truly knows what caused the crime spree, aside from the fact that Todd was a huge fan of the Grand Theft Auto game series and had been addicted to it for years. His spree replicated some aspects of the game but he was already a career criminal by that point.

Less than 10 minutes after leaving the bus, he found a haunted house attraction called *The*

Slaughterhouse, which had been established in the downtown area of the city since 1996. Despite it being closed at 3.15am, Todd decided to break into it.

No alarms were set off and so he went through the attraction finding items to steal. In one of the offices, he found a taser, a revolver, and a shotgun which he stole for use later on. On the way out, and not one to miss an opportunity, he stole a Slaughterhouse t-shirt.

He then decided to close the attraction permanently by setting it on fire and burning it to the ground. With weapons – and a Slaughterhouse t-shirt in hand – he admired his handiwork before walking away and visiting a nearby bar.

At 3.30am, realising he needed money to move up a level, he attacked four people who were leaving the bar. He held them up at gunpoint and tased one of them to show he meant business. After pistol-whipping another, he ordered the group to hand over their credit cards and cash.

Ten minutes later, he broke into a nearby parked taxi and headed to a 24-hour Walmart. While there, he loaded a trolley full of food and used one of the stolen credit cards at the express lane checkout where he spent $199. And then, things got really weird.

Shit gets weird

By that point, police were already made aware of The Slaughterhouse burning down, and the group who had been attacked. Officers didn't connect the incidents immediately, but Todd was on his way to commit another crime to add to their list.

At around 5am, after stuffing his face with the food from Walmart, he walked into a nearby law office and smashed his way through the front door. After having eaten a lot of food, he needed to expel some of it, and so he climbed up on a desk, pulled down his pants, and took a great big giant poo.

Then he picked up the faeces and smeared it all over the framed law degree certificates adorning the walls. At 6am, happy with his poo-stained artwork, he left and went to the adjacent Hotel Indigo where he entered through the service entrance.

Todd let his hair down and went to one of the rooms on the first floor. He impersonated a female housekeeper and woke up a Canadian couple who answered the door. Todd then pushed them back into the room at gunpoint and robbed them of $600 in cash.

According to the couple in a later interview, they stated that Todd was in tears the whole time he robbed them and seemed inconsolable as he went about his spree. He kept them in the room with him for around an hour before leaving and hiding in a cleaning closet.

He realised that his long red hair would make it easy for him to be tracked and so he shaved his head completely, with a razor purchased at Walmart, then dumped his hair in a mop bin before walking out of the hotel in plain sight.

Poking his nose out

Security footage showed a bald man leaving the hotel at around 8am in full view of police who were there investigating the robbery of the Canadian couple. At 9am, Todd carjacked another taxi and drove around the downtown area at high speed before crashing into a parking garage.

He stumbled out the wreck and crawled away but realised he needed to get another vehicle. After traipsing around town with a bag full of weapons, cash, and food, he climbed into another taxi and put a knife to the driver's neck.

At 11am, he ordered the driver to park up at the Opry Mills Shopping Mall, just outside of the city centre, and home to 182 stores. He left the driver in the car and entered the large building before heading to the mall's cooling tower where he found a large tank of water.

Thinking it would be a good place to hide, he put his loot under a stock cage, and jumped into the tank. Once the ripples settled, he poked his nose out the top of the water in order to breathe but the police had already been informed by the taxi driver that the madman was in the mall somewhere.

When police saw that water had been splashed out of the tank, they looked inside and saw Todd's nose sticking out. Squeezing his nose shut, they pulled him out of the water and arrested him on the spot, bringing his bizarre and madcap crime spree to an end.

More than grand theft auto

At the same time the Greyhound bus left Nashville for its next destination, and the smoke was clearing from The Slaughterhouse fire, Todd had managed to commit 11 crimes including burglary, assault, and fraud.

It emerged that Todd was also wanted in Kentucky for theft and it may have been the reason why he left for Tennessee. It was suspected that his love of the Grand Theft Auto games influenced his decision to go on a spree.

In June 2013, Todd was sentenced to three years in prison for aggravated robbery, three for arson, two for burglary, and eleven months for each of three separate assaults, with all sentences to run concurrently.

Despite his sentencing, Todd was released in 2016 and fell straight back into a life of crime. In June 2019, he went on another smaller spree, committed another robbery, caused $10,000 worth of damage, and carried out an aggravated burglary. In April 2021, he was sentenced to eight years in prison for those offences.

A conspiracy theory later emerged regarding the Nashville spree. When the Canadians in the hotel room told police Todd was crying all the time, it led some theorists to consider the possibility that Todd's body was being controlled by someone else, much like in the Grand Theft Auto games, and that the controller took his body on a crime spree – none of which is likely to ever be proven.

Whatever reason Todd decided to go on a crime spree, it remains one of the most bizarre and yet curious sprees of recent memory. That he was committed again of robbery and burglary, not long after being released from prison, shows that as a career criminal, he may never be rehabilitated.

The Slaughterhouse reopened at a new location and remains one of Nashville's most popular attractions. It remains unclear if the lawyer cleaned up his framed law certificates or opted for replacements – free of any human faeces.

FACTS!

In 2019, in the state of Tennessee, 221,800 crimes were reported, 40,000 of which were violent.

Nashville has a metro population of 1.99million, while Tennessee is home to 6.9million (2020).

A 2021 report from the University College of London (UCL) showed that people who play violent video games have a lower risk of depression. The same report suggested that social media has a more damaging effect on youth.

Deep Freeze Murder Mystery

A teenage girl is abducted, only for her body to show up a month later frozen like ice, but there are no fingerprints and no suspects, leading to one of Britain's most baffling unsolved murder mysteries.

A month after she went missing, the fully clothed body of 17-year-old Anne Noblett was found in woodland, frozen solid, despite the weather being mild, leading to a suspicion her killer had kept her on ice.

Born in 1940 during the Second World War, Anne grew up to be a quiet and shy girl who loved dance and rock 'n roll and was enrolled at the Watford Technical College. She enjoyed living with her well-off parents in Wheathampstead, Hertfordshire, where she was raised, just 27 miles north of Central London.

On 30th December 1957, the bespectacled Anne attended a dance lesson with friends at Lourdes Hall in Harpenden, four miles away from her home. After class, they all jumped on the bus headed in the direction of Anne's family home.

Anne got off the bus at Cherry Tree Corner, Marshalls Heath, close to the Cherry Trees Pub, which was only quarter-of-a-mile walk away from her home. She waved at her friends as the bus continued on its route.

A minute later, a local girl named Shirley Edwards rode past Anne on her scooter and was the last person to see her alive. At some point during the next ten minutes, between the Cherry Trees Pub and her home, Anne disappeared.

Frozen solid

Anne was reported missing the same night and the police brought in search dogs to scour the area but found no trace of the homely teenager. Her parents organised a search party the next day but to no avail despite involving an estimated 1,000 people.

A local resident told police she noticed a vehicle stopped on the lane where Anne would have walked home at the time of her disappearance, but only saw its rear lights in the dark, leading police to conclude that Anne had been abducted.

Local cinemas began showing newsreels about the disappearance before films to raise awareness, and over 2,000 statements were taken by police but they had no suspect. The case went cold quickly as no new leads were uncovered and evidence was thin on the ground.

On 31st January 1958, one month after the disappearance, RAF Airman Hugh Symonds, and his younger brother Brian, were walking the family dog through Rose Grove Woods when the dog ran off into a clearing.

The brothers followed the dog and stumbled upon Anne's fully clothed body, six miles away from her home. It appeared as though she may have been asleep but Hugh reached out and touched her body to discover that she was frozen solid like a block of ice.

Which was unusual, as the winter had been mild, and the temperature had been rising quickly into the new year. There was no natural way that the body could have been frozen unless it had been kept on ice and dumped in the days prior to the discovery.

Police arrived on the scene and confirmed that it was the missing 17-year-old. Her body couldn't be seen from the nearby lane, 200 metres away, and if the

Symonds's dog hadn't gone into the clearing then it may have remained undiscovered for longer.

Murder on ice

An investigation team arrived at the unusual scene and got to work. Anne was found fully clothed and still wearing her glasses, but her undergarments had been incorrectly buttoned up which suggested she had been sexually abused or raped.

Her purse and belongings were close to her body, meaning she hadn't been robbed, or that the killer had left the items to throw police off the scent. Coins from her purse were spread over the ground around her body.

After an autopsy was carried out, the pathologist concluded she had been strangled to death shortly after her abduction and that there were signs of sexual assault. There was undigested food in her stomach that she had eaten on the day of her abduction.

The woodland location had already been searched after the disappearance which meant her body had been placed there after the fact. The day after the body was found, the surrounding woods were searched by a bigger group of locals and soldiers to find any evidence as to who had killed her.

The nearby lane was only generally used by locals as a shortcut which suggested the killer may have been living nearby. The local Criminal Investigation Department (CID) headed by Detective Chief Superintendent Robert Elwell called in the New

Scotland Yard murder squad to help in the investigation and they began to piece together the murder.

Anne had been picked up, either by someone she knew or was forcibly abducted, then taken back to a property where she was raped, strangled to death, then placed in a large freezer where she remained until one month later. Unusually, there were no fingerprints found on Anne's body, clothes, or belongings.

The freezing of the body gave police a lot to work on. It was suspected that she was kept on ice for one of two reasons. The first being that the killer knew about the local investigation and couldn't risk dumping the body when the region was under scrutiny.

The second being that the body was frozen to confuse detectives about the timeline of her death. If her body had thawed out then it may have looked as though she had died later than she actually did. It was a tactic used by hitman and serial killer Richard Kuklinski (The Iceman) in the United States.

Baffling murder case

Police searched every house and business within a 30-mile area looking for large freezers on the assumption that it was a local person who had abducted Anne. At the same time, the press jumped on the story and referred to it as the Deep Freeze Murder.

The investigation team were looking for a strong man who would have carried Anne's 11-stone frozen body from a vehicle to her final resting place, without dragging the body through the undergrowth.

The search teams went through industrial sites, farms, outbuildings, sheds, garages, and any location where a freezer may have been placed. But of the thousands of freezers searched, not one showed any signs of having stored a dead body.

Due to the unusual method of freezing the body, the police admitted that it was one of the most baffling murder cases they had ever come across. Detective Elwell then suggested that Anne might have been kept inside a refrigerated vehicle.

There was even the slight possibility that she had been picked up by a murderous ice cream van driver who lured her into the van with sweet treats. When investigating the vehicle angle, Elwell and his team expanded the search to cover London and neighbouring counties.

But as the investigation grew in geographical size, it became harder to narrow down where they should be searching and the case began to drift away from them.

No forensic evidence

It was suggested that the body had lain in the spot for two weeks prior to being discovered, because the shrubbery around the body had two weeks additional growth than the crushed shrubbery beneath it. But the body hadn't thawed out and was still frozen, dispelling the two-week theory.

After the death, some of the local residents stated they had seen a black car driving around the area in the days prior to the abduction, driven by a man wearing big-rimmed glasses. The car and man were never traced and were never seen again. Within a couple of months, the murder investigation had gone cold.

A more recent theory suggested that the body had been dumped in a refrigerated van without the knowledge of the owner and when that owner found the body, decided to place it in the forest. The refrigerated vehicle theory remains a stretch for most researchers, as driving the body of a dead girl around the country was too bold a move for a killer in the 1950s.

All forensic evidence collected from the body was destroyed 40 years later in the 1990s due to police storage regulations at the time. Using any kind of DNA technique, including profiling, has been off the cards ever since.

A perfect murder?

In 2017, 60 years after the murder, Hertfordshire police briefly reopened the case and appealed to the public for help but to no avail. There was no new forensic material or no new evidence to shine light on a possible suspect, who police believed would have died long before 2017.

Anne's death fell into the realm of the unsolved, and that's when sightings of ghosts and tales of hauntings began doing the rounds. In the 1970s, a worker at an industrial unit near to Anne's old home, saw a teenage girl standing next to a shed, when the worker called to her, the girl vanished before his eyes.

Local cats were known to have stopped near the site of the abduction and hiss at something unseen. Other locals told tales of someone brushing up against them when no one else was around, and a nearby hire centre continuously experienced strange happenings like doors opening by themselves and cold spots in the building.

A séance was held in the late 1990s at the location the body was found and the spiritualists claimed to have received the identity of the killer but no one was arrested, let alone named.

There remains one more interesting connection to Anne's murder. 75 miles away in Colchester on 5th January 1958, just one week after Anne disappeared, 19-year-old Mary Kriek got off a bus near her home and was abducted.

Her body was found in a ditch the next day only a few miles from her home, she had been battered to death. Despite the similarities between both Mary's and Anne's deaths, detectives found no evidence to link them. Interestingly, Mary's death also remains unsolved to this day.

It appears that the case of Anne Noblett may never be cracked and remains one of Britain's most baffling unsolved murders. Her killer may have got away with the perfect murder – until his judgement at the pearly gates.

FACTS!

There are an estimated 2,600 unsolved murders in the UK, with most being female victims.

The county of Hertfordshire is one of the top 10 safest counties in the UK, with an average 2021 crime rate of 58 crimes per 1,000 people.

The town of Wheathampstead where Anne was killed is home to 6,500 people (2021).

The Devil's Night Murder of Martha Moxley

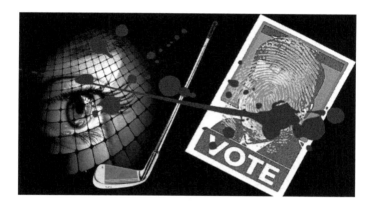

The night before Halloween in Belle Haven, a wealthy teenage girl was murdered in the night. The case went unsolved for 25 years, until a suspect was arrested – who had ties to the Kennedy family.

Greenwich in Connecticut is one of the richest places in the United States, with an average annual salary of $350,000, and property owned by people associated with large hedge funds that the area is known for.

The neighbourhood of Belle Haven is now an exclusive gated community within Greenwich that in the Seventies used to be a summer resort for wealthy travellers from New York City.

A day before Halloween, on 30th October 1975, 15-year-old high school student Martha Elizabeth Moxley was murdered in Belle Haven, which shocked the entire region. Her murder went unsolved for 25 years until a Kennedy family member was linked to the death.

Born in August 1960 in San Francisco, California, the Moxley family moved to Greenwich soon after Martha's birth and she was raised in a rich society with even richer friends but had none of the snobbery that some of her neighbours were known for.

On that fateful evening in 1975, Martha and her friends went out to take part in Mischief Night, an informal holiday a day before Halloween in which people take part in pranks, parties, or in some locations; vandalism.

Also known as Devil's Night, the tradition began in England in the late 18th Century and historically took place a day before bonfire night on the 4th of November. As it went international, the date moved away from bonfire night and ended up a day before Halloween.

In the 1970s, pranks were more about harmless fun, which included ringing doorbells and running away, throwing toilet paper into trees, and rearranging garden furniture. For a 15-year-old girl, it was the most fun to be had in a wealthy neighbourhood – until death came knocking.

Six-iron golf club

Martha's neighbours, in the house opposite, were the Skakel family, who had familial links to the Kennedy administration. Ethel Skakel was married to U.S. Senator Robert F. Kennedy and was the sister-in-law of President John F. Kennedy.

Ethel's nephew, Michael Skakel, who was 15 at the time, would eventually be convicted of Martha's murder, which sent shockwaves through the political sphere. Prior to the murder, Martha had been seen by friends flirting with 17-year-old Thomas Skakel, Michael's brother.

They were last seen at 9.30pm kissing behind the fence of the Skakel residence, beside their large swimming pool. Her friends left them to it and went back to their own homes. When Martha didn't return home that night or the next morning, her family became concerned.

At 12pm on Halloween, one of her family members found her body beneath a tree in their backyard. She was nude from the waist down and had been beaten to death with a six-iron golf club, pieces of which were found beside her body.

An autopsy concluded she had not been sexually assaulted but had died from a combination of being beaten with the golf club and stabbed with a sharp section of it as it broke over her skull. Within a few hours, police traced the golf club to the Skakel residence, and were told to tread carefully due to the family's connection to the Kennedy's.

Fermenting in the graveyard of the unsolved

Martha's friends confirmed they had last seen her with Thomas the night before which made him the prime suspect. But Thomas's father refused to give police access to his private school or his medical records. Thomas later passed a lie detector test which ruled him out as a suspect.

The family attempted to push blame onto a new live-in tutor named Kenneth Littleton, who had started work for the family the night of the murder but police could find no evidence linking him in any way.

Despite knowing that Martha was with Thomas the night of the murder, and despite tracing the murder weapon to the Skakel household, no-one was arrested or charged with the murder, and the case was left to ferment in the graveyard of the unsolved.

Martha's friends and family were convinced that one of the Skakel's had murdered her and living opposite them became a headache for all concerned. Three years later, after a drink-driving incident, Michael was sent to a private school in Maine that specialised in teaching young people with mental health and drug problems.

While there, it is claimed he admitted to killing Martha many times but the release of that information was either covered up or ignored as fanciful tales. As the years passed, many books and articles were written about the murder but still no one had been arrested and Michael was convinced he was getting away with it.

Then in the Summer of 1998, 23 years after the murder, and after a book by Mark Fuhrman pointed the finger at Michael, a one-man grand jury was convened to review the evidence. The new investigation vowed to uncover the truth of the murder in Belle Haven.

Skakel conviction

In his original statement when he was 15, Michael claimed that he had gone to a cousin's house to watch a film and returned home about 11.30pm.

Various private investigations in the years after the murder all seemed to point to Michael as the killer with only some convinced that Thomas was the culprit. Both brothers changed their alibi's and stories over the years hoping no one would notice but many detectives believed Michael was the killer.

During the grand jury investigation, Kenneth Littleton gave evidence in exchange for immunity and claimed that Michael had lied about his whereabouts that night. Another pupil at the school Michael went to claimed that Michael said he would get away with murder because he was a Kennedy.

18 months later in January 2000, 25 years after the murder, Michael surrendered to authorities when he heard a warrant was out for his arrest. Three months later, he was charged with the murder and sent to a juvenile court due to his age at the time of the incident, but in January 2001, a judge ruled he would be tried as an adult.

A year later in May 2002, the very public trial began, and lasted three months when in August 2002, Michael was found guilty of murder and sentenced to 20 years to life in prison. He maintained his innocence and continued to claim he had been at a cousin's house that night. Despite the conviction, campaigns to release him increased, leading to a continuation of the story.

The circus continued

There was no forensic evidence to prove that Michael had killed Martha, and he was convicted on the basis of circumstantial evidence and witness statements. In 2003, Robert F. Kennedy wrote an article damning the trial and claimed there was no more evidence against Michael than there was against many others that night.

He blamed the 'inflamed media' for stoking the fires of the trial and forcing the jury's hand. Kennedy also believed that Michael had been framed for the murder as an attack on the Skakel/Kennedy families but offered no other reason as to why they were targeted beyond their political links.

In 2007, Michael's lawyers made an appeal for a retrial based on new evidence. Video logs from a private investigation in 2003 showed that Gitano Bryant, cousin of basketball player, Kobe Bryant, admitted that one of his friends wanted to rape Martha. The appeal was thrown out.

Another appeal in 2012 failed to reduce his sentence, and his first parole hearing that same year was also denied. In 2013, after 11 years in prison, Michael was granted a new trial based on the fact that his lawyer at the time was more interested in collecting money and fame than keeping him out of jail.

In November 2013, Michael was released on a $1.2million bail bond with various restrictions in place. In 2016, the murder conviction was reinstated on a majority decision based on what the court called 'overwhelming evidence.'

In 2018, the circus continued, when prosecutors requested to the Supreme Court that Michael be returned to prison to continue his sentence but another appeal at the same time managed to convince the court that the original trial was unfair.

In October 2020, it was made public that Michael would not be retried, and he walked out of court as a free man, 21 years after his conviction, and 45 years after Martha's murder.

Guilty or not?

Martha's family still believe that Michael killed her and despite being released as a free man, they believe that justice was done, due to the amount of time Michael spent behind bars.

There have long been two sides to the story. On one hand are the Skakel/Kennedy family who strongly believe that Michael is innocent, which they say is demonstrated by the fact that the courts could not prove within a reasonable doubt that he was guilty.

The other camp believe there was enough evidence against him to prove he was the killer, and as a 15-year-old boy from a wealthy family, believed he would get away with it. But the biggest question that has never been answered throughout the entire affair was simply; what was the motive?

In 2021, a documentary finally dug deeper to reveal the missing link. Martha's friends and diary revealed that Michael had an explosive temper and was known to be competitive with Thomas in their professional and private lives, especially when it came to girls.

A leaked document was released in 1995 from a private investigation ordered by Thomas and Michael's father to prove his family innocent – which it didn't. The report proves that Michael lied about his whereabouts.

After returning from his cousin's house, he felt horny and climbed a tree outside Martha's window where he proceeded to masturbate. He then claims that he blacked out and woke up in his own bedroom unaware of what had happened. It was the same tree where Martha's body was found.

The motive was most likely rejection when Martha turned down his sexual advances. He was jealous of his brother for getting close with her and wanted her all to himself. The most damning piece of evidence was an audio clip.

In it, Michael is heard speaking to a researcher of a new book when he mentions being awoken by Martha's family members to find out where Martha was. He said to the researcher that only one thought crossed his mind; *'oh my God, did they see me last night?'*

And yet, even to this day, the case is pulled around, twisted, screwed up, and thrown out to various theorists and those convinced either way whether Michael was guilty or not.

But at the heart of this story is the brutal murder of a 15-year-old girl, who had her whole life ahead of her. A victim whose story is mostly side-lined in favour of the monster who took her from the world, whether it was Michael or someone who has never been named and remains hidden in the shadows of Belle Haven.

FACTS!

The average house price in Belle Haven comes in at $2.4million (2021).

From 1616 to 2005, 126 people were sentenced to death and executed in Connecticut. The death penalty was abolished in the state in 2012.

There have been an average of 110 murders each year in Connecticut since 1970.

The Casino Killer and the Bad Samaritan

A teenager killed a young girl in a casino restroom and pushed her body into the toilet, minutes after his friend walked in on the attack – and did nothing.

Casino's attract a wide range of people and can be fun and dangerous at the same time. Some put down their entire wage packet while others enjoy a small flutter like they would on a national lottery, if enjoyed the right way and within personal limits, a casino can be an experience like no other.

On 25th May 1997, Labor Day weekend, Leroy Iverson took his seven-year-old daughter, Sherrice, and her 14-year-old half-brother, Harold, to Primm, Nevada for a break away. Their mother, waitress Yolanda Manuel stayed at home in Los Angeles.

That evening, Leroy went to the Primadonna Resort and Casino to play slots and blackjack. Leroy wasn't addicted to gambling but enjoyed a bet every now and again, never normally winning big on the tables. Still, it was a pastime that suited him.

With no one to look after his children, Leroy took them to the casino with him. His son stayed with him most of the time but Sherrice was younger and wanted to play, as she had dressed up in a sailor outfit. On at least two occasions that evening, officials in the casino led Sherrice back to Leroy to look after.

But within minutes of being led back each time, Sherrice would run off to the video game section or play with adults who noticed her. One of those adults who took great interest in Sherrice was 18-year-old Jeremy Strohmeyer.

Little girl outfits

Born in 1978, Jeremy was raised in a damaging environment. His birth parents were both drug addicts and had a history of mental illness between them. His mother had been diagnosed with chronic schizophrenia and had been hospitalised at least 50 times.

Jeremy was taken into state care at a young age and adopted by new foster parents in Long Beach, California. They were never informed of why he had been removed from his parents, nor that they were suffering from combined drug and mental health issues.

As such, Jeremy had a predisposition for mental illness but it didn't excuse his future behaviour. Despite his parentage, he found it easy to get girlfriends but had a fetish for dressing them up in little girl outfits to satisfy his sexual appetite.

On 25th May, Jeremy and his 17-year-old friend, David Cash, and David's father, paid a visit to the Primadonna Resort and Casino, wearing baggy shorts and t-shirts. It wasn't long before Jeremy set his sights on Sherrice, taken by the young girl's playfulness and sailor costume.

At 4am, while Leroy was busy gambling, Jeremy asked Sherrice to play hide-and-seek with him. Later when detectives viewed the CCTV footage, it seemed entirely innocent; a young man playing with a young girl.

Nothing seemed overly untoward, until Jeremy told Sherrice that the only place she would be safe to hide was the ladies toilets. Not knowing what was to come, Sherrice ran away from Jeremy and hid where he had suggested. A few minutes later, making sure no one was looking, Jeremy followed her into the restroom.

Rape and murder

Still acting as though he was Sherrice's friend, he played a game of throwing wet paper towels at each other. But it was no game, Jeremy was luring her slowly to the disabled cubicle. He suddenly grabbed her and held his left hand over her mouth, while sexually groping her with his right.

At that moment, the door swung open and David walked in, wondering what his friend was up to. Jeremy shook his head at David as if telling him to keep it quiet and leave. David watched Jeremy groping Sherrice before he left them to it.

Jeremy then shut the door to the disabled cubicle and raped Sherrice. While she was being attacked, two women entered the restroom, so he began squeezing Sherrice's neck to keep her quiet. When the women left, he strangled her to death because she could identify him.

When he went to leave the cubicle, he noticed that she was still breathing, and wanted to make sure she was dead like they did in the movies. He reached an arm around her neck and squeezed hard in an attempt to break it.

When he heard a popping sound and her head twisted sharply, he knew the deed had been done. He then folded her body in half and squashed her feet first into the toilet bowl, before walking out as if nothing had happened.

Emotionless

Sherrice's body was found an hour later, the sight of which caused the local sheriff to call it the most gruesome case he had ever worked on. Video footage of Jeremy was put out to the press, and his college friends recognised him immediately, but David still hadn't said a word about what he had seen.

Jeremy was arrested as he attempted to flee through his backyard, and was quickly charged with first degree murder, kidnapping, rape, and sexual assault. When the arrest hit the news, commercial airlines refused to fly him back to Nevada and a private jet had to be arranged.

Due to his adopted family's wealth, Jeremy knew how to fly a plane, and instead of talking to officers about the murder, he joked about plane crashes and shared his knowledge about the airline industry. The officers escorting Jeremy referred to him as emotionless and nonchalant about the murder he had committed.

At the trial, Jeremy's defence attempted to place the blame on David, who had turned witness for the prosecution. They claimed David was the real murderer, and that Jeremy was high on drugs at the time, both of which were never proven.

It was discovered that Jeremy's biological father was in prison for drug and assault offences and his biological mother had been admitted to a long-stay psychiatric hospital, which the defence attempted to use as a reason for Jeremy's behaviour.

Not willing to risk a death sentence, Jeremy pleaded guilty to first-degree murder, first-degree kidnapping, and two separate sexual assaults on a minor. In September 1998, he was sentenced to life imprisonment without the possibility of parole. But the furore had only just begun.

The Bad Samaritan

The public were outraged that Jeremy was not sentenced to death despite pleading guilty. During the pre-trial, Jeremy insinuated he had killed Sherrice because she was black, and because he was white he would be able to get away with it, which led to death sentence campaigns rising up around the country.

For his own protection at the maximum security Ely State Prison, Jeremy was moved to a special isolated cell away from the general population, as rumours were flying around that some inmates wanted their own revenge for the crime he had committed.

Sherrice's family suggested that David be charged as an accessory to the murder as he was seen going into the ladies restroom after Jeremy. But there was no evidence to suggest he had taken part in the murder, and his deal with the prosecution to turn witness meant he couldn't be charged.

After a series of interviews in the press, where David confessed he wasn't going to lose any sleep after Sherrice's death and that he was going to make money off the back of the trial, he was referred to as The Bad Samaritan.

Human responsibility

David never expressed remorse over what happened but his inability to stop his friend attacking a young girl became a cause of concern. Campaigns were created to have him removed from his university but they fell on deaf ears because the truth was that David hadn't committed a crime, at least not a criminal one.

There is no general law in the United States or United Kingdom that requires people to report a crime or stop a crime in progress. However, Nevada later passed a bill that required people to report a crime where a person under the age of 18 is being sexually or physically abused. A similar law was passed in California but for those under the age of 14.

Interfering in a crime is considered a moral judgement personal to the witness in question. The new laws meant that if the incident happened again then David could have been charged with not reporting the crime. To this day, the law remains controversial and is rarely invoked.

Despite numerous appeals, Jeremy remains incarcerated but was moved to a medium security prison. His adoptive parents attempted to sue Los Angeles social workers for withholding the drug and mental health issues of his birth parents. They failed but remain supportive of their adopted son.

Many people will never be confronted with witnessing a crime such as the Sherrice rape and murder and will never have to face the decision of whether or not to intervene. But the hope remains that moral judgement and human responsibility may outweigh the guilt of simply letting it go.

FACTS!

In 1997, there were 187 murders recorded in Nevada.

The population of Nevada has tripled in 33 years from one million in 1987 to three million in 2020.

In 2019, there were 3,286 robberies in Nevada, the lowest on record since 1990.

The Eyeball Eater

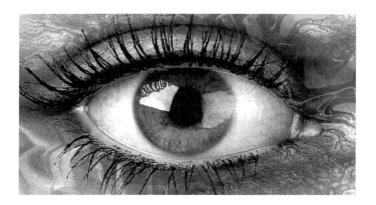

The case of a crazed man who slaughtered his entire family, cut open their chests, removed their hearts, and gouged out his own eyeballs – before eating one of them.

The story of Andre Lee Thomas reads like something out of a horror novel, with elements of violent murder, mutilation, hallucinations, and self-cannibalisation. Except, this story is far from being a fictional tale we can hide from with the lights on.

Born in 1983, Andre was raised by his mother with five brothers in Sherman, Texas, near to the Oklahoma border. They were a poor family, never having enough money to pay the bills, and relying on handouts from the state.

Andre's mother was an alcoholic who suffered from various mental health issues including depression after being abused as a child and later in her adult life. The family had already suffered after Andre's uncle was shot dead by his father-in-law.

By the age of 10, Andre was known to be suffering from hallucinations and delusions which had seemingly come out of nowhere. He often told friends that he heard the voices of angels and demons arguing inside his head and couldn't get rid of their voices.

He later claimed he was the real person behind one of the characters in the Mortal Kombat video game, so much so that he had developed an unwritten history of his life within the game and the circumstances that led to his image being used.

When he was 14, he had already survived two suicide attempts and been arrested multiple times for theft and disorderly behaviour. Despite being placed on suicide watch many times, he received no mental health help – something which would come back to haunt the city of Sherman.

The voice of God

At the age of 15, Andre started a relationship with a white girl called Laura Boren, who became pregnant with his child when she was 14. They named him Andre Jr. and married when Andre was 18 but split up shortly after when Laura had a daughter by another man.

In the months leading up to the murder, and suffering from the fallout of the marriage, Andre's already obvious mental health condition began to deteriorate further. He began to believe he was hearing the voice of God in his head.

Because God told him not to talk for days at a time, he put duct tape over his mouth to silence himself, only removing the tape to smoke marijuana and drink alcohol to help him quiet the voice in his head, which never went away.

He also harmed himself with various implements which put him in hospital multiple times but he would check himself out before receiving any psychiatric treatment. Andre had been forced to live alone after his ex-wife took the children and moved in with her new boyfriend.

The loneliness combined with ill mental health and inability to pay bills became too much to bear. In early March 2004, a few days before the murders, Andre stabbed himself in the chest and was rushed to hospital, claiming he was attempting to cross over into Heaven. He left before being committed to psychiatric care.

Gruesome murders

Two days later, on 27th March 2004, Andre waited for Laura's boyfriend to go to work then kicked down the door to their third-floor apartment and stabbed her in the chest multiple times. As she fell to the floor, he broke through her ribcage with the knife and cut her chest open before removing a portion of her lungs.

Not content with viciously murdering the mother of his child, he moved to the children's bedroom where he stabbed four-year-old Andre Jr. and Laura's one-year-old daughter to death. After their blood splashed the walls of the room, he opened their chests and removed their hearts.

He then went back to Laura and laid down next to her body before stabbing himself three times in the chest. After a few minutes, he realised the stab wounds were non-fatal and decided to walk home with the children's hearts in his pockets, later stating he believed he was in hell.

After he told his family what he had done, he surrendered himself to the Sherman Police Department. He told officers that his three victims were possessed by demons and that he cut them open to mix their blood together in order to save their souls.

Five days after the murders, while in a cell awaiting trial, Andre used his fingers to gouge out his right eyeball. When officers entered his cell, the eyeball was on the floor next to him, and he was reciting verses from the Bible claiming he had removed his eye because of his sins.

Self-cannibalisation

He was diagnosed with schizophrenia and spent many weeks in a hospital before his trial which began in February 2005. Despite being mentally ill, Andre – a black man – was put on trial in front of an all-white jury, many of whom were openly against interracial marriages.

The prosecution convinced the jury that Andre's insanity defence should be ignored as his mental illness was made worse by drug use. The jury found him guilty of three murders and he was sentenced to death.

Three years later while on death row in Texas, his condition had worsened and he claimed to see tiny demons coming out the walls and playing music to him. He cut his own throat with the side of a plate but survived the suicide attempt.

An appeal in October 2008 upheld the original conviction and reaffirmed that Andre was not insane at the time of the murders. Two months later, on 9th December 2008, Andre ripped his left eyeball out – and ate it, blinding himself completely.

He told doctors he ate his left eye so that the government would not be able to read his thoughts. After he was discharged from hospital, he was sent to an institute that housed prisoners with mental health issues. It was the first time in his life that he would be cared for by mental health professionals.

In 2015, a human right's group suggested that Andre's self-torment was punishment enough and condemned the death sentence and lack of help. In

April 2021, after another appeal claiming the original defence was ineffective, the original verdict was upheld yet again, and Andre was to remain under a death sentence indefinitely.

Unsurprisingly, Andre's case caught the public's attention and raised questions over what exactly constitutes mental health and an insanity plea. It remains certain that a mentally healthy person would not rip out their eye and eat it on the orders of a hallucination.

FACTS!

In 2004, 1,364 murders were recorded in the state of Texas, and has remained at around that level ever since.

Sherman, Texas, has a population of 43,000 (2020).

The city was founded in 1846 and named after General Sidney Sherman, a hero of the Texas Revolution that ended ten years prior.

The Ossett Exorcist Murder

A loving husband, thought to be possessed by 40 demons, became the subject of an all-night exorcism, and less than two hours later; ripped his wife and dog to pieces with his bare hands.

*E*xorcism turned loving husband into killer! A true case of possession! The Ossett exorcist murder! So read the headlines in 1974 England, when 31-year-old Michael Taylor killed his wife by tearing her eyes and tongue out with his bare hands, following an exorcism by a local team of priests.

Born at the tail-end of the Second World War in 1944, Michael was raised in the English market town of Ossett in Wakefield, West Yorkshire. Though Ossett was very much a Christian town, the Taylor family were not overly religious and never found the time to attend the local churches.

Neighbours of the family described them as mild-mannered and full of kindness, despite their unwillingness for a religious life. Michael became a full-time butcher and married the love of his life, Christine, soon after.

By the early 1970s, the couple had five children and were living in a small rustic house in the town they'd both grown up in with their dog. Michael hurt his back in an accident that forced him to leave the butcher's job and struggled to find full-time employment afterwards.

He suffered bouts of depression which saw him becoming withdrawn from the community and he became less social with those around him. This caught the attention of one of his friends, Barbara Wardman, who believed the only cure for his depression was religion.

Carnal desire

Barbara introduced him to a church group called the Gawber Christian Fellowship, despite Michael not attending church regularly. He attended the first group meeting with Christine, and both were so impressed with the group's outlook on life that they converted straight away.

When Michael's depression began to improve after a number of group meetings, his friends and members of the church believed it had improved purely on the basis of spiritual intervention and by the hand of God himself.

While at the church meetings, Michael became besotted with the 20-year-old lay preacher, Marie Robinson. A lay preacher is a preacher or religious servant who is not a formally ordained cleric and helps the church in the promotion and function of its beliefs.

Within a few months, their friendship had reportedly become 'carnal' – another way of saying they were intimately engaged. Marie's soft spoken leadership of the group was too much for Michael to ignore and he spent as much time with her as he could.

Soon enough, Marie held private meetings with Michael, where he would supposedly talk in tongues and made the sign of the cross with his hands for hours on end, believing it would quieten the dark and evil power of the moon; the opposite to the light and goodness of the sun.

Michael began joining in some of the sermons and helped cast out demons from other group members, even though neither Marie nor Michael were trained exorcists. They were simply using their positions to empower themselves.

A few weeks later, members of the group met at Michael's home, and Christine voiced her opinion that

Michael was spending too much time with Marie. Michael then forced Marie upstairs where she rejected his advances before re-joining the group.

The exorcism

When Marie rejected him in his own home, Michael's attitude changed and he became argumentative with Christine at every opportunity. He withdrew back into depression, acted irrationally and developed a bad attitude towards the church group.

Then Michael attacked Marie in full view of the group. He rose from his seat, and stared at her with wild, bestial eyes, and a look of a man intent on killing. Marie began screaming out of fear at the sight of him but Michael grabbed her by the shoulders and neck and shouted at her in tongues.

Marie called upon the name of Jesus, and the other members of the group managed to restrain Michael, who had no memory of what had gone down. Concerned he was becoming possessed by a demon, the congregation called on a local priest and his wife to intervene.

Peter and Sally Vincent invited Michael to their home for an assessment where Michael threw their cat out of a window and broke some pottery in anger. After witnessing his anger and actions, the Vincent's put together a team of people to help in an exorcism at the church.

On 5th October 1974, as the midnight hour dawned, Michael was summoned to St. Thomas Church where he was restrained and underwent a seven-hour exorcism. Peter and his team burned Michael's crucifix, pushed wooden crosses into his mouth, doused him with holy water and screamed at him to dispel the demons.

At the court case following the murder, Peter confirmed they had exorcised a total of 40 demons who had taken residence within Michael. Coincidentally, the only demons they couldn't exorcise were those associated with murder, violence, and insanity.

Ripped at and left in a mess

The priests told Michael not to worry about the other three demons and that they would exorcise them at a later date, so he was sent home. Less than two hours later, a policeman on a routine patrol through the town stumbled on a gruesome sight.

Michael was ambling along the street completely naked and covered head to toe in blood, screaming about the demons within him and Satan himself. The officer managed to restrain Michael and took him to a hospital, before heading to Michael's home where more police were outside.

Their neighbours had heard violent noises and already called police. When the officer arrived, a senior detective stumbled out the house and vomited in the front garden, telling him not to go inside as Christine Taylor had been ripped at and left in a mess.

In a possessed rage, Michael had killed his wife by tearing at her face and chest with his bare hands. He ripped out her eyes and tongue, and according to the autopsy report, had almost ripped off her entire face from her skull.

He had then strangled the family dog to death before tearing its body to pieces, ripping its limbs off and covering himself in its blood, along with the walls and floor. When Michael was arrested in hospital, he claimed that '*the evil inside her had been destroyed.*'

Torment of the exorcism

In an unprecedented trial, Michael was acquitted on the grounds of insanity. A defence psychologist posited the theory that Michael's actions were a direct result of the intense psychological torment he had suffered at the exorcism, and laid blame on the priests involved.

The priests who were brought in to testify stated they had expelled all but three of the demons and it was one of the three demons that had possessed Michael and used his body to kill Christine. Though the trial didn't prove that Michael was possessed, it did lead to him being acquitted.

Michael was sent to the infamous Broadmoor psychiatric hospital for two years before being transferred to a lower-security facility for another two. He was released just four years after brutally murdering his wife and dog.

If any of this sounds familiar, the case was mentioned in the 2021 film *The Conjuring: The Devil Made Me Do It*, which is based on the 1981 trial of American murderer Arne Cheyenne Johnson, who claimed he was possessed by a demon.

The case was investigated by demonologists Ed and Lorraine Warren, who believed that Arne was indeed possessed. Arne was ultimately convicted of manslaughter and spent five years in prison. Demonic possession was never proven.

The exorcism of Michael Taylor raised many public questions that were never answered including why the priests in charge of the exorcism had never been charged with psychological damage, or why Michael was released only four years later.

Whether he was possessed, psychologically tortured, mentally unstable, or a cold-blooded killer, depends on one's own beliefs of the existence of the otherworldly, and that which can inhabit a human body and mind.

In 2005, Michael was arrested again for touching a teenage girl, and was admitted to psychiatric care – with the same symptoms as he had showed in the hours before he ripped his wife apart. Leading some researchers to suspect that a demon remains within him still.

FACTS!

Canon 1172 of the Code of Canon Law states that no priest can legitimately perform exorcisms unless he has obtained 'express permission' from the local bishop.

Since 2017, exorcisms in the UK, France, Italy, and the United States have been on the increase.

The Vatican holds annual exorcism courses and trains around 250 priests a year.

Case of the Missing Nun

While out shopping, a nun from a convent in Wales vanished without a trace, leading to an enduring mystery that has never been solved, and yet she wasn't the only nun who disappeared that year.

Sister Jacinta Bracken was once described by a fellow nun as '*a dear little creature with a lovely soul, dreadfully shy to the point of being timid.*' It was in response to a theory that Jacinta had orchestrated her own disappearance, which would have been odd, and yet her case is odder still.

38-year-old Jacinta was born Christina Nuala Bracken in the village of Gorteen, in Ballacolla, Ireland, and moved to Wales to start a new life as a nun where she showed her commitment and devotion to the Lord Saviour by choosing the new name of Sister Jacinta Bracken.

On Saturday May 19th 1979, Jacinta began her day like any other at Swansea's Stella Maris Convent. She awoke at 7am in her small room then dressed and washed. After communal prayer, she ate some cereal, and made herself a cup of tea.

She spent the rest of the morning marking homework from the class she taught during the week. After lunch, she helped with kitchen duties and then decided to head into Swansea city centre to buy her mother a birthday gift.

Before she left, she asked another nun if she wanted to walk into town together but the nun still had duties and agreed to go for a walk in the evening when she returned. But in the same month as Margaret Thatcher became Prime Minister, Sister Jacinta vanished from the face of the earth.

The last people to see her alive

When Jacinta failed to return to the convent, the other nuns raised the alarm and the police were called in. It was instantly an unusual case, as stories of nuns going missing were incredibly rare which led police to believe something untoward had gone down.

On May 20th, a boatman found Jacinta's handbag which contained the birthday present she had bought for her mother. When police were informed of the discovery, a major missing persons investigation got underway.

The handbag also contained a pair of stockings and some cash which discarded robbery as a motive if something criminal had taken place. When police searched Jacinta's room, they found a ferry ticket to Ireland and a small amount of savings in cash.

When the story hit the press, it took over the headlines for many days, leading to witnesses coming forward to claim they had seen her. Various people had seen her walking alone through the suburb of Uplands and claimed there was nothing troublesome about her.

Two young teenagers, who Jacinta taught in her class, saw her near the Quadrant Shopping Centre car park in the middle of Swansea city centre the afternoon of her disappearance. They were, by all accounts, the last people to see her alive.

Welsh Detective Jenny Brain was brought in to oversee the case and kept in constant contact with the convent for many weeks after. She later confirmed that no one at the convent believed Jacinta had left of her own accord, leading Brain to believe she may have been abducted.

One witness came forward to claim Jacinta was praying in the city's St David's Roman Catholic Church the evening of her disappearance but the witness couldn't see the person's face. The case of the missing nun rose more questions than answers.

The theories

The first theory was that she had returned to Ireland but her ferry ticket was in her room at the convent and she had left all of her personal belongings. Her handbag had been found on the beach near the West Pier on the South Docks, which at the time was a disused wasteland with abandoned industrial units.

The riverbanks were so badly managed that the beach was covered with swathes of wet mud at low tide. And yet the area wasn't unknown to Jacinta, she would sometimes take the coastal route on her way back to the convent.

Another theory rested on a homeless man in the city who Jacinta had befriended. He was known to be aggressive towards the public and had been seen with her many times. When police searched for him after the disappearance, he was nowhere to be seen – he too, had vanished.

Detective Brain looked at the possibility Jacinta had been sucked into a hole on the dock wall caused by the varying tides, on the basis of a clairvoyant's vision that Jacinta had fallen into the docks after being hit by a rogue wave.

Brain sent police divers into the dock wall but they claimed there was too much suction around it and it was dangerous for them to have gone in deeper. If

Jacinta had been sucked into a hole on the dock wall then her handbag would have been too, and it wasn't, it was found on the beach untouched.

The area has now been filled in and is an upmarket marina. Apart from the handbag, there was no physical evidence of what happened to Jacinta. In the decades that followed, her National Insurance number was never used and her passport remains unrenewed.

Vanished into thin air

It remained unlikely that Jacinta would have forsaken her religious vows and vanished to start a new life in anonymity, for there was no reason for her to have done so, and no change in her schedule or personality suggested she was going to elope.

Detective Brain was so convinced of foul play that the case of the missing nun has never been closed and the investigation still acts on any new information it receives. Only one month after Jacinta disappeared, and 3,300 miles away in New York, another nun vanished without a trace.

On June 26th 1979, in Schenectady County, 37-year-old former Franciscan nun Agnes Shoe disappeared and was reported missing by her husband after he returned home to find that she had not left any food or water for their dog.

Like Jacinta, she had no reason to disappear and was living a happy and fruitful life. She remains a missing persons case but investigators have long worked on the suspicion that she had been met with foul play.

Though it may have been a coincidence that two nuns of a similar age vanished without a trace within a month of each other, both cases remain connected by some researchers. The truth is that neither nun has ever been seen alive again.

In 2005, Detective Inspector Andy Hughes made a fresh appeal for information relating to Jacinta's disappearance, as the case has never been far from the public eye. A reconstruction of Jacinta's last movements were aired on the BBC but concluded with no new leads.

Despite many private investigators looking at the case, there has been no trace of the homeless man who befriended Jacinta – and no trace of Jacinta herself. It's as if she simply vanished into thin air. Her surviving family members have never given up hope that the truth will one day come out.

FACTS!

Around 250,000 people go missing in the UK each year, with approximately 99% being located.

Swansea has a metro population of 462,000 (2016) and is the second largest city in Wales behind the capital Cardiff.

On average, 25 women a year in England and Wales take the vows to become a nun.

The Beasts of Satan

Bonded by their love of death metal and occult rituals, the Beasts of Satan went on a six-year killing spree involving sacrificial murder, drug-fuelled sex, and Satanism.

A death metal band and sect called the Beasts of Satan went on a six-year killing spree from 1998 to 2004 in Milan, Italy, that left at least four people dead. They were suspected of being involved in 14 deaths and disappearances in total.

'Blood and death, blood raining down, blood bathing all my body, blood thirsty for blood. Madness is always one of the risks, it's necessary to maintain concentration on hatred.' – notes written by leader of the Beasts of Satan, Nicola Sapone.

In the centre of Milan was a rock and heavy metal club called the Midnight Pub. It was a place where the Beasts of Satan had played and where they decided upon their victims. It was well known throughout the city as a popular establishment for rock and metal fans.

The members of Beasts of Satan took their stage act literally when they began killing friends and fellow musicians. After all was said and done, seven people were convicted of the murders, including Beasts of Satan band members Nicola Sapone, Paolo Leoni, Marco Zampollo, and Eros Monterosso.

The other three were another band leader Andrea Volpe, his girlfriend, Elisabetta Ballarin (an upper-class teenage runaway) and colleague Pietro Guerrieri. An eighth suspect, Mario Maccione was acquitted as he played a secondary role in the crimes.

Dancing on the graves

Their wave of brutality began in January 1998 when 19-year-old Chiara Marino and her 16-year-old boyfriend Fabio Tollis, who was a one-time lead singer for the Beasts of Satan, were lured from the Midnight Pub to their deaths under a full moon.

They had spent most of the night drinking in the pub but failed to return home the following morning. The group took the couple – who were their friends – to remote woodland near to Somma Lombardo and took lots of drugs.

In a drug-fuelled frenzy, they stabbed Chiara in the heart as part of an occult ritual they had found in old books, then beat Fabio to death with a hammer. It was claimed that the killers had sex with Chiara before and after her death.

They buried the couple's bodies deep in the woods then danced on their graves, mocking the dead and laughing about what they had done. The investigation into the couple's disappearance was closed when detectives concluded they had eloped as lovers.

Fabio's father, Michele Tollis, realised something was untoward and refused to believe the investigation's conclusion. He discovered his son's connection to black and death metal bands, and his love of Satanism. In fact, Michele would become instrumental in bringing the band and cult to justice.

He spent the next six years privately building his own case against them. He put together mountains of paperwork and files about the Beasts of Satan, the member's lives, their friends, and their involvement in other disappearances and murders – while the official investigation stuttered.

Satanic sect

In January 2004, Volpe and his girlfriend Elisabetta, summoned Volpe's ex-girlfriend, 27-year-old shop assistant Mariangela Pezzotta. They told her to meet them at a small chalet in Golasecca, a small town in Italy known for its ancient burial customs

Volpe had already decided to kill Pezzotta, as she knew too much about the first murders and other murders that were later connected to the Beasts. As the couple raised their champagne glasses and toasted to their health, Volpe shot Pezzotta in the throat with a shotgun.

He got on the phone to Sapone to ask for help in burying the body but suddenly realised that Pezzotta was still alive – barely. When Sapone arrived, he mocked Volpe by saying that he couldn't even kill a girl. Volpe and Sapone then mutilated Pezzotta and crushed her skull in with a spade.

Pezzotta was still alive when she was partially buried in the greenhouse of Elisabetta's family home to incriminate her family who she hated. Just a few hours later, Volpe and Elisabetta took a large amount of cocaine and decided to get rid of Pezzotta's car.

They planned to sink it in a nearby river but because they were so high on drugs, they crashed into a wall and were arrested when police arrived. Surprisingly, Volpe confessed to the murder and the double murder in 1998.

After Pezzotta's murder, Michele Tollis took his six-year long findings to the police, who used them to link all three murders to Andrea Volpe and the Beasts of

Satan, and for the first time uncovered the Satanic sect connection that had evaded them before.

Links to more deaths

The aforementioned eight people were arrested and charged in connection to the three murders. When the investigation looked closer at Michele's files they realised that the sect could have been responsible for up to 14 deaths in total.

In September 1998, Beasts of Satan drummer Andrea Bontade took his own life by driving his car into a wall, after other band members psychologically abused him and pushed him to suicide, saying he didn't have the guts to do it.

Between 1998 and 2004, in and around Milan, many others had either disappeared, taken their own lives, or been killed in a violent manner, who were connected directly or indirectly with the Beasts of Satan.

In December 1999, friend of the group and cemetery caretaker Angelo Lombardo was burned alive while attending to some of the gravestones. A year later in December 2000, death metal band member Doriano Molla was found hanging by his neck in the woods, in what was thought to be a murder. Other alleged victims were also found hanging, had disappeared, or been burned alive.

The first trial took place in 2005, Volpe got 30 years, and Guerrieri, 16. At the second trial in 2006, Sapone was sentenced to life, with Leoni, Zampollo,

Monterosso and Elisabetta, sentenced to between 24 to 26 years each. A 2007 appeal saw all but Elisabetta's sentences increased.

Death metal is not the enemy

The Beasts of Satan were so reviled in Italy that their crimes were referred to as one of the most shocking crimes in post-war Italy. The authorities considered that the Beasts of Satan may have been part of a wider network of Satanists within the country but no evidence was found.

At the time, Italian officials were concerned by the rise of occult practices and notions being pushed on young people. A Milan-based priest publicly called for black and death metal to be banned, blaming the music for being an instrument of evil.

Enjoying death metal is no worse than watching horror films or playing horror video games. In one psychological study, many fans of death metal reported feelings of transcendence and positive emotions. It was the naysayers and non-fans of death metal who expressed anger and hatred at the music.

Those involved in death metal tend to be creative, smart, and mostly kind human beings. The music and performances are an act and outlet like any other stage act, song or movie. One can listen to dark lyrics and horror-based works because there is a lack of real-world consequences – it's not real.

However, dark creative arts in any format may influence those who already have a predilection towards violence and chaos. Those like the Beasts of Satan, took their love of the art literally and decided to kill because they enjoyed the act of murder and were appeasing what they believed was a greater evil.

The Beasts of Satan made an impact in Italy that has never been forgotten. Some of the convicted have since been rehabilitated and released, but they may never be able to escape the true darkness of their past lives – ones that sent innocent people to the grave and beyond.

FACTS!

Satanic panic is a term associated with ritual abuse and murders relating to satanic worship, beginning in the United States in the 1980s and spreading to the rest of the world in the 1990s.

More than 12,000 documented accusations of satanic ritual abuse have been recorded since the 1980s, including many unsolved murders. .

Milan has the highest crime rate in all of Italy, with almost 5,000 cases per 100,000 inhabitants.

The Mormon Manson

A polygamous cult leader ordered the murders of at least 25 people, many from beyond the grave, in a tale of fear, control, and a mission to create the Kingdom of God on Earth.

Children of cult leader Ervil LeBaron claimed they were taught to live in awe of their father as he was a self-proclaimed prophet of God and the one true prophet on Earth. They were taught that they were celestial children, whose destinies were to follow in Ervil's footsteps.

Except, not all was peachy in Ervil's church. Many of his wives were married to him when they were underage, and he was known to abuse his children and other members of the group. He also ordered mob-style hits against his rivals or those who stood against his cult.

The *Church of Jesus Christ of Latter-day Saints* (Mormon Church) banned polygamy (more than one spouse at the same time) in 1890 but has been tarnished with the trait ever since as they never entirely removed it from their doctrine.

At that time, those Mormons who believed polygamy was their right, split from the church and moved to Mexico to avoid U.S. Law. In 1924, Alma LeBaron Sr., who believed in polygamy, moved his two wives and eight children to North Mexico where he started a farm and commune called Colonia LeBaron.

When Alma died in 1951, leadership was transferred to his son Joel LeBaron. Joel was able to circumnavigate U.S. law and incorporated the community as the *Church of the Firstborn of the Fulness of Times* in Utah.

His younger brother, Ervil LeBaron, was second in command for a short time and split his time between the Utah group and the new Baja Peninsula group; Los Molinos. In the late 1960s, Ervil fought for control of the group, leading to membership of the group splitting into two factions.

God then apparently ordered Ervil to split from his brother's leadership and form his own church in San Diego called the *Church of the First Born of the Lamb of God*. It was then that God apparently told Ervil to start killing people.

Ervil's kingdom

On August 20th 1972, Ervil ordered his followers to head back down to Mexico and kill Joel, as God had told him to do so. Two followers carried out his wishes and killed Joel by beating and shooting him. Two years later, in Mexico, Ervil was tried and convicted of Joel's murder but an appeal overturned his conviction on a technicality – though some suspect the courts were bribed.

Joel's death was the first in a long line of murders and crimes associated with Ervil's cult. In retaliation for Ervil having gone to trial, his followers descended on Los Molinos and destroyed the commune, killing two more men in the process.

Realising he could gain more power – or on the word of God, as he put it – Ervil turned his attention to Mormon leaders of other groups who held polygamous views. In April 1975, minster Bob Simons, known for teaching Native Americans, was killed on Ervil's orders.

In 1977, Ervil ordered his 13th wife and her daughter to kill leader of the *Apostolic United Brethren*, Rulon C. Allred. They killed him without question and later claimed in a book that Ervil was using mind control and fear to keep his followers loyal.

Ervil turned his attention to killing his own family members whenever they showed intentions to leave his cult. He ordered his 10th wife, Vonda White, to kill follower Dean Glover, as he had attempted to leave. Vonda was later sentenced to life in prison for the murder, in addition to being suspected of another killing.

The self-proclaimed prophet of God also ordered the murder of his own 17-year-old pregnant daughter, Rebecca LeBaron, as she asked if she could leave the group to raise her second child. But if the murders were bad enough, it was made worse when Ervil began ordering kills from behind bars – and beyond the grave.

The Book of the New Covenants

The church moved around to avoid detection from the law and split their time between the U.S. and Mexico. But the law was already onto the cult. Ervil was arrested in 1979 and ultimately sentenced to life in prison in 1980 for ordering the death of Rulon Allred.

Despite his conviction, his remaining followers still believed he was the one true prophet on Earth and waited for instructions. While in prison, Ervil wrote a new bible called *The Book of the New Covenants*, which contained a commandment ordering followers to kill those who wish to leave or didn't follow orders.

20 copies of the bible were printed and distributed among his followers. Little did the prison guards know that inside the bible was a list of names of people that Ervil claimed had gone against God and his cult and needed to be killed.

Ervil died of apparent natural causes in the summer of 1981 but his followers were still active. Two days after his death, Verlan LeBaron died in a suspicious car accident in Mexico City. Seven years later, in 1988, the cult struck again.

At exactly 4pm on June 27th 1988, four murders were committed simultaneously in Texas. One of Ervil's former followers, Duane Chynoweth, who had escaped the cult many years earlier, was shot dead with his eight-year-old daughter as they ran errands.

Ervil's stepson, Eddie Marston, was killed as he walked down a local street. And at the same time, father of six Mark Chynoweth was shot multiple times as he sat in his office in downtown Houston. It appeared that Ervil had the power to order murders from beyond the grave.

The Mormon Manson

The Texas murders became known as the 4 O'clock Murders, and over the next two decades, five people were convicted of them, including one of Ervil's daughters. Much of the testimony and documents given during the LeBaron trials were sealed by the courts.

The Book of the New Covenants has never been publicly released but some members of the LeBaron family had it digitized many years ago. Some of Ervil's children carried on his teachings claiming that his way was the right way, and that it was their mission to establish the Kingdom of God on Earth.

Some of the dead have never been accounted for and additional victims linked to the LeBaron cult continue to appear. In 1989, six of Ervil's children left various foster homes at the same time in an organised escape and were suspected to have rejoined the cult in Mexico, with rumours a refuge still exists somewhere in the country.

In 2017, one of Ervil's daughters, Anna LeBaron, told her story to the BBC. She told how the cult would move from one safehouse to the next and that they slept on filthy floors and lived off food that had been thrown away by nearby residents.

She explained how Ervil had all of them under a grip of terror and that they would have to do everything he asked for fear of being murdered. He taught them that the outside world didn't understand them which is why they had to keep moving around to avoid the law.

The young children of the cult were beaten for showing any sign of attitude or anger towards Ervil. Female marriage age in the LeBaron family was set at 15 but came with allowances to marry younger girls should they be the right fit. Ervil was known to have married some of his wives at such a young age.

An estimated 25 to 30 people were murdered on the orders of Ervil LeBaron, whether in person or posthumously, and his cult legacy continues to be felt today. In the land of cults, the LeBaron family sit head and shoulders above the rest, leading some elements of the media to have labelled Ervil as the Mormon Manson.

FACTS!

Members of the Church of Jesus Christ of Latter-day Saints are not allowed to drink coffee or beer.

Some Mormons are considered 'preppers' as they store a year's worth of food, water and money in case of emergencies.

Polygamy is illegal in all 50 states in the U.S. but in 2021, Utah reduced the felony category from a third-degree crime to a minor infraction.

Angel's Landing Cult

An evil cult leader, claiming to be an angel, slept with children to fix them and keep himself alive, and collected life insurance policies when his followers began dying in suspicious accidents.

Angel's Landing was the name given to a 20-acre compound near Valley Center and Kechi, outside of Wichita, Kansas. The commune was led by Lou Castro who held power over his followers by making them believe he was an angel and seer who could travel into the future.

He could tell his followers how they were going to die using his angelic powers. He also told them he was hundreds of years old and needed to have sex with children otherwise he would die, leading to the repeated rapes of dozens of children.

His rape victims ranged from the age of eight to 16, and he was later convicted of multiple offences from 2001 to 2011. He was also linked to the suspicious deaths of six adults whose life insurance policies were claimed by the cult.

Investigators were aware of the commune but struggled to pin down exactly what was going on. The Angel's Landing cult moved from state to state, making it difficult to track exactly what they were doing. It was only while based in Kansas that an investigation could look deeper.

Angel's Landing had been investigated since 2006 but nothing solid could be pinned on them, and yet it was their unexplained wealth that opened the doorway for authorities to finally take a closer look at the cult.

Suspicious deaths

Castro did not work but most of the vehicles on his commune were new and expensive, with most cars worth over $40,000. There was no paper trail leading to their purchases which made it difficult for investigators to go about their business.

There was a luxury swimming pool and multiple houses on the commune which would not have come cheap. In 2003, when Castro settled on Kansas as his base, he brought another family into the fold, the McGrath family, including 15-year-old Sara McGrath, 11-year-old Emily, and their mother, who was a real estate agent who helped Castro secure the large property.

Sara claimed that her mother had a bond with him that she didn't understand, and she took an instant dislike to Castro, who raped her on regular occasions as part of the cult's indoctrination and to keep the angel within him alive. In June 2003, Sara was informed by Emily that one of the commune's followers had mysteriously died in the swimming pool.

Cult member Patricia Hughes had apparently slipped and fallen into the swimming pool and drowned. Her death had been predicted by Castro in the exact manner that she died. The death alerted the authorities to the commune but still had no evidence to move in and find out what was going on.

Patricia's widowed husband, Brian, became depressed and spoke to Castro about his feelings and future, when Castro told him that he would have his chance to see her again on the other side. Castro travelled to the future and predicated that Brian would die in a vehicular accident.

Three years later in 2006, Brian died in a freak accident at an auto-shop where he was working on his car. When the death appeared to be suspicious,

Wichita detective Ron Goodwyn took on the case and dived into the inner workings of Angel's Landing.

No accident

Almost immediately, Goodwyn struggled, as there was no information or records of Castro. For the other cult members, he managed to dig up personal and financial data and began building a profile of the group.

He even went as far as following Castro to local restaurants then digging through the trash afterwards to find a fingerprint. Then Goodwyn uncovered the potential source of the cult's funds; Castro had collected a $1.24million life insurance pay-out from Patricia Hughes's death, and another £1million from Brian's death.

It seemed the accidents were no accidents at all. In 2011, a year after Castro moved from Kansas to Tennessee, a Kansas-based witness came forward and said that she saw Castro get into the pool with Patricia and drown her. Castro ordered the then 12-year-old-girl to wait 20 minutes while he drove into town to create an alibi for himself.

After 20 minutes, she was told to jump into the pool in an attempt to 'save' Patricia on the basis she had fallen into the pool while rescuing her dog. For nearly a decade, the abused girl had to live with the 'guilt' that she couldn't save Patricia when she had already been killed by Castro.

In a bizarre twist, Castro later claimed that Patricia had given herself to the cult and agreed upon her death so that the group could cash in on her insurance. Detective Goodwyn had motive for the accidental deaths and accusations of rape but still had no idea who Castro was.

A wanted child abuser

In 2010, Castro moved from Kansas to Tennessee and created a new identity for himself in an effort to evade the law, under the name of Joe Venegas. Shortly after moving to the state, Castro was arrested for identity theft and fraudulent use of a Social Security card number.

He was charged and sentenced to two years in prison, which gave the FBI and Detective Goodwyn enough time to dive into his past lives. They used witness statements from the abandoned followers to piece together his life.

It appeared that Lou Castro didn't exist, and that his real name was Daniel Perez, a Texan who was on the run from state police after being charged with sex crimes against two underage girls. When the survivors of the cult began to open up and talk to the FBI about what had happened at Angel's Landing, Goodwyn saw the extent of Perez's crimes.

One witness who was only 11 at the time, said that she submitted to Perez sexually and mentally as she lived in fear of her life and the life of her family, some of whom were not followers of Angel's Landing.

Other interviews with cult members suggested that up to six people had died in suspicious accidents from 2001 to 2010, and in each of the cases, Perez had claimed their life insurance on behalf of the cult, amounting to approximately $7million over a period of nine years.

Manipulative

In addition to providing Perez with an income, his predictions of the deaths helped convince his followers that he truly was a seer and angel. Perez was taken back to Kansas in 2014, where his trial began a year later.

He was convicted on one count of first-degree murder, one count of sexual exploitation of a child, three aggravated assaults, seven aggravated sodomies, eight counts of rape, and eight counts of making false statements, though he was charged with more rapes and involvement in the deaths of some of his followers.

In February 2015, he was sentenced to two life terms and would be eligible for parole in 2095, aged 134, which means he's likely never getting out of the Lansing Correctional Facility in Kansas. Perez was no angel, nor a seer, but managed to convince dozens of people he was, purely to make money off their deaths and sleep with their children.

Alongside claiming that sex with children would keep him alive, he told his young victims that he was fixing them. Perez was an evil cult leader, a manipulative abuser who committed atrocious crimes in the name of God purely for his own sick desires and will be remembered as such.

FACTS!

According to various reports, women make up at least 70% of all cult members worldwide.

There have been an average of 115 murders each year in Kansas since 2001.

In 2019, almost 80,000 crimes were reported in Kansas, the lowest since 1972.

Justice For All

When an abused woman reported her partner to police for assault, she never expected to become instrumental in solving the murder of a young girl twenty years earlier.

I n April 2001, while sitting in the waiting room of a courthouse in Winchester, Hampshire, Michelle Jasinskyj nervously awaited the moment she would be called up to testify against her husband, in a domestic violence case that had left her with broken ribs.

Michelle had married Tony Jasinskyj, nine years her senior, in 1988, and went on to have six children with him as the years passed. Soon after their marriage, Tony changed and became violent and aggressive towards her, accusing her of cheating, and controlling her every move.

Tony was an army chef and had been based at the Aldershot army barracks before leaving and taking on a job as a security guard. He attended the Desford Free Church and maintained the image that he had a perfect family life.

In early April 2001, while washing the dishes one night, Michelle found the courage to tell Tony she was leaving him. Asserting his violent control, he came up behind her and punched her in the side of the head, knocking her to the ground.

As she fell, he continued his barrage of punches and kicks and shouting at her all the curse words under the sun. After Tony retreated to the lounge, and despite having broken ribs, Michelle crawled to a neighbour's house where the police were called.

Tony was charged with assault, and a routine DNA swab was taken. A few days later, while waiting to testify against him, Michelle was sitting in the court waiting room, nervous about facing her abuser again, and worried what the future might hold.

A police officer entered the room and Michelle thought the time to testify had come – but the officer had news that was going to change her life forever. Tony's DNA had been run through the database and he had been arrested on suspicion of the rape and murder of a 14-year-old girl, 20 years earlier in 1981.

Canal murder

On Saturday 6th June 1981, 14-year-old Marion Crofts left her home in Basingbourne, Hampshire, to ride her bike to band practice at Wavell School, North Camp, five miles away. It was a route she had taken many times before, and her parents, Trevor and Anne, were confident in her own cycling ability and safety.

Marion was the youngest of three daughters and played clarinet in the band. Most Saturdays, Trevor would drive her to the school but on that fateful day he was due to play in a cricket match at around the same time.

The route took Marion along a part of the Basingstoke Canal, on Laffans Road in Aldershot. Between 9.30am and 10am, she was pushed off her bike and dragged into a small, wooded area beside the road, where she was beaten unconscious.

As she lay dying, the attacker raped her then brutally beat her around the head until she appeared to be dead. A later medical examiner's report concluded she had died from bleeding on the brain caused by massive head injuries.

Her broken body was discovered by a police dog handler later the same day. Her bike and clarinet had been thrown into the Basingstoke Canal and were later recovered by specialist divers. Despite DNA testing in its infancy, forensics collected semen from inside and outside Marion's body.

There were also traces of semen found on her jeans. It was the collection and storage of evidence that would ultimately lead to the capture of Tony Jasinskyj. The material was stored in the belief that technology would advance to such a point that the killer could be found.

The case went cold

In the days following the murder, which shocked the area, the police compiled a list of thousands of suspects, including Tony, but due to a lack of evidence at the time, no one was charged.

The murder of Marion Crofts went cold and ended up on a list of cold case investigations that would only reopen once new leads came in. Though they were not closed cases, they only saw movement if police received a tip or new evidence.

However, due to the police having the forensic material, they planned to input the data into the police database once a year, every year, until the killer was identified. Because of the brutality of the murder, the case didn't stray far from the minds of the investigators involved in it.

In the weeks and months following the murder, Tony began to believe he would get away with it. At the time of the incident, he was based with the Army Catering Corps in Aldershot, only a mile from the murder scene.

Almost all of the military personnel on the base were added to the suspect list but were later removed due to not enough physical or circumstantial evidence. Tony was interviewed and questioned by police about his whereabouts the time of the murder but lied his way out of it

Due to the amount of suspects, the work required to physically check each of them was overbearing and many were crossed off as a matter of routine.

Tony was married at the time and his first wife had no idea what he had done. He divorced her in 1984 and discharged himself from the army. He moved to Leicester, became a security guard, and married Michelle, hoping to escape the horror he had committed on the Crofts family – but the past never forgot.

20 years later

It was Tony's penchant for violence and desire to control others that would ultimately lead to his downfall. When Michelle had gone to the police, she would have had no idea that in some way, she would become responsible for catching a killer.

In 1999, two years before Michelle pressed charges against Tony, police had managed to create a DNA profile based on the forensic material collected from the murder scene. The forensic material had been kept sealed until such time that DNA technology had caught up, so there was no possibility of cross-contamination.

They checked the DNA against the National DNA Database on a regular basis until they got the hit they were waiting for. They discovered that Tony had been arrested for domestic violence and assault and that a routine DNA swab had been taken, leading to the match on the database.

There was no disputing it, Marion's rapist and killer had finally been found, 20 years later. Tony denied the charges and was sent to trial where he pleaded not guilty to rape and murder.

The prosecution proved that the DNA lifted from Marion's body was a one-in-a-billion match for Tony. In 2002, he was sentenced to life for murder and an additional ten years for rape, despite his defence claiming the evidence was flawed.

Justice for all

Justice finally came for the Crofts family, 21 years after Marion's murder. Though their suffering and pain wouldn't entirely come to an end, they would all sleep better knowing that her killer was finally behind bars.

In 2014, Tony and his defence team launched an appeal on the basis that the original trial was flawed because the DNA suggested the killer had a chromosome disorder, which he didn't have. Unsurprisingly, the appeal for wrongful conviction failed.

For Michelle, who lived for years in fear of the violence from her husband, she too could sleep better knowing he was behind bars. But the horror of finding out her husband was a rapist and murderer would never go away.

When her children began asking if they shared the blood of a murderer, she told them to be masters of their own destinies and step away from the shadow of their father. Michelle sat next to Marion's parents when the verdict was read out and they all cheered at the outcome.

If it wasn't for the bravery of one woman standing up to her abuser and reporting him to police, then perhaps Marion's murder would have never been solved and her killer would have never been caught.

FACTS!

In England and Wales, for the year ending March 2021, there were 613,000 cases of domestic abuse related incidents reported to police.

There are an estimated 3,000 cold cases in the UK at any given time, and 285,000 in the United States.

The overall crime rate in 2021 for Hampshire, UK, was 80 crimes per 1,000 people, one of the highest in England and Wales.

Halloween Murder of Collette Aram

A confident killer murdered a 16-year-old girl and escaped justice for 25 years until advancements in DNA technology captured him, in the first case to be profiled on Crimewatch.

On the last afternoon of her young life, 16-year-old trainee hairdresser Colette Aram spent the time preparing and baking cakes at her family home in Keyworth, Nottinghamshire, a large village six miles from the centre of Nottingham.

At 8pm on 30th October 1983, Colette left home to visit her boyfriend's house. He normally picked her up from her house but his car had been taken off the road as it required work. The 1.5mile walk normally took about 25 minutes, but by 10pm, when Colette hadn't arrived, the alarm was raised.

Phone calls were made between her boyfriend and family before they realised something bad must have happened. Fearing Colette had become involved in an accident, her family and friends began searching for her along the route but the cold bite of the October night proved a hindrance.

Police put out a missing person's report and suspected she may have visited a friend's house but all her friend's told them they had not seen her. Though her family thought an accident may have happened, they were not prepared for the truth.

At 9am on Halloween morning, Colette's naked body was found in a field a mile away from where she had been abducted. She had been raped and strangled to death, with her body posed in a sexually provocative manner.

Crimewatch

When the missing persons case turned into a murder investigation, police increased their manpower and began seeking information from locals. Colette had last been seen ten minutes after leaving her home when she stopped and talked to a group of friends.

Ten minutes after, a resident in a nearby house remembered hearing a woman scream but was unsure if it was kids messing around or a genuine cry for help. The resident remembered hearing a car drive off immediately after.

Crime scene investigators collected as much evidence from the scene of the crime as they could, which would help them in the future when DNA technology had advanced. At the time, police had little to go on, with only minimal forensic evidence, no direct eye-witnesses to the abduction, or a suspect.

The case went cold quickly much to the public's anger and put Keyworth on the map for all the wrong reasons. Nine months later, in June 1984, the BBC released the first episode of a crime reconstruction and appeal programme called Crimewatch.

Colette's murder was notable for being the very first case to be featured on the show. The format of Crimewatch was to reconstruct as much information of a crime as possible, in the way that was agreed upon by police.

As a result of the programme, Nottinghamshire Police received 400 calls, some of which claimed to have seen a car leaving the village at high speed. The programme allowed police to eliminate over 1,500 suspects.

But aside from wiping the suspect list, and various other tips, most of the calls led nowhere and the killer had seemingly got away with it. The case was run a second time on Crimewatch's 20th Anniversary show in 2004, but again, the case was already as cold as ice.

Never say never

The killer was 25-year-old Paul Stewart Hutchinson, a youth worker who had a liking for young girls. On the day of the murder, he had spent hours in a shed near a riding school close to the village, waiting for girls to start walking home alone.

His heinous plan was to lure one of them into the shed and rape them. He had already approached two girls that morning who told their families a man had acted strangely around them. It was reported to police only after the murder became public knowledge, but by that point, Hutchinson was long gone.

When he failed to select a victim, he stole a Ford Fiesta and drove around the country lanes, hoping to find a girl walking out in the darkness alone. At around 8.20pm, he pulled up next to Colette and proceeded to speak to her before jumping out of the car and abducting her at knifepoint.

He bundled her into the back seat of the car and smashed a bottle over her head before driving to a secluded location and raping her. He then hit her with the bottle multiple times before strangling her to death.

After killing her, he moved the body to the middle of a nearby field and posed her body, for reasons that never became known. Many suspect he was attempting to trick police into thinking he was a serial killer and that if he posed the body a certain way, the police would be looking for someone else.

Hutchinson didn't stop there, and out of a morbid curiosity, had returned to the village to watch the police investigation amidst the supposed anonymity of the crowds on 31st October, while wearing a Halloween mask.

A few days later, he sent a letter to police that read; *'No one knows what I look like. That is why you have not got me. You will never get me.'* For many years, the letter proved to be true but under the old adage of 'never say never', justice would finally catch up with him, 25 years later.

Unusual hit on the DNA database

To cover his tracks, Hutchinson told his family he had cancer, and shaved his head, blaming it on chemotherapy, which was a lie. In the years that followed, Hutchinson believed he had escaped justice, and was able to work with children with learning disabilities.

In 2008, and because of advances in DNA technology, police were able to use the carefully protected forensic evidence from the crime scene and put together a DNA profile of the killer. At the same time they appealed for members of the public to report anyone they thought might have been involved in the murder.

The appeal didn't work but in June 2008 the DNA database returned a hit – which immediately didn't make sense. A man called Jean-Paul was arrested on a traffic offense and a DNA swab was taken at the police station.

His DNA was a near-identical match to the murder suspect profile drawn up by forensics. The police had their man, after 25 years, they could finally seek justice for Colette's murder, except, Jean-Paul had been born five years after the murder took place which instantly ruled him out.

The DNA match provided police with the clues they needed to solve the case and learned that Jean-Paul was the son of Paul Stewart Hutchinson, which is why the DNA profiles were so similar. Police arrested the then 50-year-old Hutchinson at his home the same day.

But Hutchinson, ever the confident murderer, had already developed a story to get the police off his scent. He claimed that the true suspect was his own brother who had passed away six months earlier and had been cremated.

Fortunately, for police, the hospital where his brother was staying before his death had taken blood samples, which didn't match the DNA profile of the killer. Hutchinson still pleaded not guilty but changed his plea to guilty on the advice of his lawyer.

The passage of time

In January 2010, 26 years after Colette's murder, Hutchinson was convicted and sentenced to a minimum of 25 years, one for each of the years he believed he had gotten away with murder. A week after his murder, Crimewatch returned to the case.

With the new evidence and killer behind bars, Crimewatch put out a new show featuring the case. In it, they were able to retrospectively look at the inconsistencies with their original programming and point out errors that had been made.

They also discovered errors in the media's reporting of the murder, including that Hutchinson was a psychology graduate, which he wasn't. Some of the inconsistencies in their programme may have resulted in Hutchinson getting away with the murder at the time.

Ten months after his conviction, and suffering from depression, Hutchinson took an overdose of prescription medication and was found dead in his cell on 10th October 2010.

For Colette's family it was a heavy blow as it appeared Hutchinson had chosen not to live out his punishment. They were also hoping he would one day confess to the murder and explain why he had taken away their loved one, as he had never given a reason.

Colette's case shows that despite the passage of time, justice will inevitably find a way, and those who have committed historical crimes will forever be looking over their shoulders.

FACTS!

Nottingham's crime rate in 2021 was 113 crimes per 1,000 people, making it one of the most dangerous cities in Nottinghamshire.

Over 14,000 cases of violence and sexual offences were reported in Nottingham during 2021.

The BBC cancelled Crimewatch in 2017 due to declining viewership.

Bank Robber and the ATM

Dressed in camo gear but forgetting to put his mask up, a robber held up a bank for $150 before depositing the three-figure haul into his account – via the ATM outside the same bank.

There are mastermind bank robbers, evil geniuses if you will, those who pull off a seemingly remarkable theft and never get caught or if they do the loot is long gone. And then there's McRoberts Williams, sometimes known as Orin M. Williams.

On Saturday morning of December 11th 2021, 44-year-old Williams entered the Wells Fargo Bank located at 3215 Old Capital Trail, Wilmington, Delaware, with one plan in mind; to rob the bank of exactly $150.

The bank was filled with customers due to shortened branch hours as well as other locations of Wells Fargo being closed on Saturdays. There were plenty of witnesses to what happened next, with some unsure as to what exactly had gone down.

When the 25-year-old female bank teller called Williams over, he already appeared to be suspicious. He was wearing military-style camo gear with a hood, except he took the hood down when he approached the counter and forgot to put his mask up.

He handed the bank teller a note that read, 'This is a robbery, I need $150.' At first, the teller believed it to be a joke but then Williams said he was sorry and that he only needed that amount.

The teller then handed over the money and waited until he had left before pushing the emergency distress button at her counter. But Williams hadn't gone far. As soon as he got outside the bank, he deposited the loot into his own bank account at an ATM on the outside of the building.

Mind control

When police arrived and looked through the security footage, they were shocked and a little amused that Williams had literally put the money back into his own account via the ATM connected to the bank he had robbed.

And yet, Williams was still a bank robber and a team was put together to hunt him down. After his ATM deposit, Williams fled the scene and went to the nearby Prices Corner Shopping Centre, just 100 feet away, where he sat on the steps on the outside of the building.

Troopers from Delaware State Police eventually arrested him behind the shopping centre, without incident. They found no cash no him as he had deposited it at the bank, but they did find a Wells Fargo bank card, which later proved he had put the money into his own account.

But Williams had an excuse and a bizarre story to tell, that in some way explained his actions, at least to mental health experts who eventually managed to speak to him. He had travelled to Delaware from his home state of California by riding on the exterior of a cargo train by hanging off the ladder on one of the carriages.

He then claimed he mind was being controlled by an unidentified third party via an organic implant located somewhere in his body. He couldn't identify the person or group who had implanted it but they had controlled his mind and forced him to rob the bank.

World's worst bank robber

After witness statements were taken and the obvious evidence was built against Williams, he was charged with second-degree robbery and held on a $6,000 bail bond – only $5,850 to go on top of his $150 haul.

He was sent to the Howard R. Young Correctional Institution in Wilmington which is known as the Gander Hill Prison due to the neighbourhood in which it is located. Though he was one of 1,500 male prisoners, Williams was then admitted into mental health care.

It was clear from the way in which he carried out the robbery that Williams wasn't entirely mentally stable. The fact he had deposited the money straight back into his own account a few metres away from the crime scene meant that he was either foolish, of ill mental health, or desperate.

Though there is no likely possibility that his mind was being controlled by external forces via that chip in his body, Williams seemed to believe it to the degree that he was to use it as his defence.

Williams was no genius robber, there was no remarkable theft, and he was certainly no mastermind. It was unusual to have deposited the money directly into his account via the ATM outside the crime scene but even more unusual that he stole only $150.

Despite his mental incapability, Williams is right up there with some of the world's worst bank robbers – and there are plenty of them. Whether he was being controlled by a third-party or just wanted enough money to keep his account in credit, his bank robbing days are long over.

FACTS!

Since 2011 in Delaware, there have been an average of 20,000 thefts each year.

The state of Delaware had the 13th lowest murder count out of all 50 states in 2020, with 73 murders. But were the 18th highest based on population with 7.4 murders per 100,000 people.

Delaware has one of the lowest state populations in the U.S. with only 989,000.

Bonus material

Bitesize Extras

Strap-on attack!

In Vero Beach, Florida on April 6th 2022, 18-year-old salesperson Victoria Marson was waiting for a package from Amazon when her 50-year-old father took delivery of it.

Not realising it was for his daughter, he opened the package to discover a strap-on sex toy inside, which surprised the hell out of him. He confronted Victoria about the contents of the package which enraged her.

She grabbed the dildo and walked away but her father tried to grab her. Victoria then beat him by punching him in the face and kicking him as he fell to the ground.

She shouted at him, '*I'm going to kill you. I hate you*,' before leaving the family residence with the dildo in hand. When her father came around, he called the Indian River County Sheriff's Office.

When police arrived, they discovered it wasn't the first time he had been physically hurt by his daughter. They arrested Victoria within the hour and charged her with domestic battery, a misdemeanour which meant she was freed the same afternoon.

Burglar leaves paint tracks to his location

On May 23rd 2003, 22-year-old Albert Jackson Dowdy decided to break into a home in Grants Pass, Oregon, and he had the perfect plan – which went terribly wrong.

Upon approaching the property, he saw a sliding glass door window and thought it would be the easiest way in. He picked up a nearby full tin of white paint and threw it against the window with all his might.

The paint tin bounced off the window, crashed to the floor and split open, splashing white paint all over Albert and the ground around him.

Not one to be put off, he managed to get into the property via another window but had already made the mistake of stepping into the paint and treading it throughout the house.

Albert made off with a grand haul of a can of tuna and a box of porridge. When police arrived, they found that Albert had left a trail of white footprints leading away from the property.

They followed the paint to a nearby budget motel and caught Albert red-handed with half the tuna in his mouth. He was charged with first-degree burglary, theft, and criminal mischief.

Man who robbed bank to escape wife was sentenced to house arrest

In June 2017, in Kansas City, 70-year-old John Ripple walked into a branch of the Bank of Labor and robbed the joint, just metres away from Kansas City Police Headquarters.

He handed a note over to the bank teller demanding money while showing them a gun and ended up stealing $3,000 in cash. But instead of making his getaway, he strolled calmly to the front steps of the bank and sat to wait for police.

When police interviewed him, John stated that he would rather be in jail than at home with his wife. This was due to his depression following a heart bypass two years earlier. John knew that a bank robbery meant a long prison sentence.

Except, the court viewed the robbery as a cry for help, and the vice-president of the Bank of Labor requested leniency due to John's mental condition. Prior to his bank robbing days, John had lived a normal law-abiding life.

His plan of getting jailtime to escape his wife backfired when the judge sentenced him to house arrest along with three years of probation, community service, and a small fine. Which meant that John was right back where he started.

Bibliography

A selected bibliography and resource.

Auther, Jennifer. (1999) Adoptive parents of convicted killer sue social workers. CNN.com http://edition.cnn.com/US/9910/27/strohmeyer.suit.01/

BBC News. (2006) Italy jails five Satanic killers. BBC News. http://news.bbc.co.uk/1/hi/world/europe/4669944.stm

Biography.com (2017) Biography of Marvin Gaye. A&E Television Networks, LLC. https://www.biography.com/musician/marvin-gaye

Black News. (2018) Man Who Brutally Raped and Killed 7-Year Old Black Girl Seeks Parole. Blacknews.com https://blacknews.com/news/man-who-brutally-raped-killed-7-year-old-black-girl-sherrice-iverson-seeks-parole/

CBS News. (2012) Man commits more than 10 felonies in 9 hours. CBS News/Crimesider.

Charlton, Corey. (2015) Leader of Kansas commune that collected millions in life insurance payouts from dead members is found guilty of drowning female member in swimming pool. The Daily Mail (UK).

Choiniere, Alyssa. (2021) Daniel Perez Now: Where Is Cult Leader 'Lou Castro' Today in 2021? Heavy.com https://heavy.com/entertainment/2020/08/daniel-perez-now-lou-castro-today-2020-update/

CJIS Data, Nashville Criminal Court Clerk. (2022) Record Check Search Criteria: Todd, William. Davidson County, Tennessee. https://sci.ccc.nashville.gov/Search/CriminalHistory Date of Report: 4/14/2022.

Cramer, Marc. (1979) The Devil Within. W. H. Allen/Virgin Books. ISBN13:

9780491023665.

Demetriou, Danielle. (2005) Beasts of Satan's killing spree has Italy transfixed.   Independent.
https://www.independent.co.uk/news/world/europe/beasts-of-satan-s-killing-spree-has-italy-transfixed-486599.html

Edwards, L.F. (1957) The Famous Harrison Case And Its Repercussions. Bulletin of the History of Medicine, 31(2), 162–171.

Fuhrmann, Mark. (1999) Murder in Greenwich. HarperCollins. ISBN13: 9780061096921.

Gaye, Frankie. (2003) Marvin Gaye, My Brother. Backbeat Books. ISBN: 0879307420.

Irish Examiner. (2006) Fresh bid to find disappeared nun. Irish Examiner. https://www.irishexaminer.com/news/arid-30261307.html

LeBaron, Anna. (2017) The Polygamist's Daughter. Tyndale House Publishers. ISBN13: 9781496417558.

Leslie, Gaby. (2012) Coach tripper William Todd commits 11 offences in wild nine-hour spree. Yahoo News.

Levitt, Leonard. (2004) Conviction: Solving the Moxley Murder. Regan Books. ISBN: 0060544309.

McAfee, David. (2021) Racist views of jurors not sufficient to overturn death sentence. Bloomberg Law.

Noonan, David. (2018) Dissecting the Bloodthirsty Bliss of Death Metal. Scientific   American.
https://www.scientificamerican.com/article/dissecting-the-bloodthirsty-bliss-of-death-metal/

Ohio State Journal. (1878) Body Snatching in Ohio. The Ohio Historical Society.

Ottawa Free Trader, The. (1878) A Body-Snatching Horror. Ottawa, Illinois. https://www.newspapers.com/clip/7256852/john-scott-harrison/

Record Check Search Criteria: Todd, William – D.O.B.: 12/2/1987

State of California. (1984) Marvin Gaye Death Certificate. http://www.autopsyfiles.org/reports/deathcert/gaye,%20marvin_dc.pdf

Suslak, Anne. (2017) Anniversary appeal for information on Wheathampstead teenager murdered 60 years ago. The Herts Advertiser.

Tipperary Live. (2012) Family appeal for long lost sister. Iconic Media. https://www.tipperarylive.ie/news/local-news/130643/Family-appeal-for-long-lost-sister.html

Turner, Steve. (1998) Trouble Man: The Life and Death of Marvin Gaye. Michael Joseph. ISBN: 0718141121.

Wheeler, Brian. (2017) Anna LeBaron: How I escaped my father's murderous polygamous cult. BBC News. https://www.bbc.co.uk/news/magazine-38526255

Whiteley, Jerrie. (2021) Sherman's only death row inmate seeks Supreme Court appeal. Herald Democrat.

Photo and Image credits:

Mohamed Hassan, Annalise Art, Colleen ODell, Flash Alexander, Music HQ, John Bergman, Paul Barlow, Dev Benjamin, Gordon Johnson, Daniel Barnes, Ben Lambert, Stefan Keller, Dalton Smith, Engin Akyurt, Andrew Martin, Prettysleepy Art, Kalea Morgan, Erol Ahmed. Designs by Twelvetrees Camden.

Images are used as a representation of the story content and do not relate specifically to the crime. Images in the public domain: Amityville house, Wakefield Prison, Robert Maudsley, Marvin Gaye, Motown House, Robert Berdella, and the 1887 illustration by British artist Hablot Knight Browne of "resurrectionists" stealing dead bodies from a graveyard.

Look for more in the Bizarre True Crime Series from Ben Oakley & Twelvetrees Camden

OUT NOW!

Fancy TWO true crime books for FREE?

Visit www.benoakley.co.uk and download today!

Printed in Great Britain
by Amazon